IN SYSTEM

Bloom's

GUIDES

David Guterson's
Snow Falling
on Cedars

1984
All the Pretty Horses
Beloved
Brave New World
The Crucible
Cry, the Beloved Country
Death of a Salesman
Hamlet
The Handmaid's Tale
The House on Mango Street
I Know Why the Caged Bird Sings
Lord of the Flies
Macbeth
Maggie: A Girl of the Streets
Ragtime
The Scarlet Letter
Snow Falling on Cedars
To Kill a Mockingbird

Bloom's

GUIDES

David Guterson's
Snow Falling
on Cedars

Edited & with an Introduction
by Harold Bloom

CHELSEA HOUSE
P U B L I S H E R S
A Haights Cross Communications Company

Philadelphia

© 2004 by Chelsea House Publishers, a subsidiary of Haights Cross Communications.

A Haights Cross Communications ⭐ Company

Introduction © 2004 by Harold Bloom.

First Printing
1 3 5 7 9 8 6 4 2

Library of Congress Cataloging-in-Publication Data

David Guterson's Snow falling on cedars / edited and with an introduction by Harold Bloom.
     p. cm. — (Bloom's guides)
Includes bibliographical references (p.) and index.
  ISBN 0-7910-7877-9
  1. Guterson, David. Snow falling on cedars. 2. Washington (State)—In literature. 3. Japanese Americans in literature. 4. Trials (Murder) in literature. [1. Guterson, David. Snow falling on cedars.] I. Bloom, Harold. II. Series. PS3557.U846S653 2003 813'.54—dc22
                              2003023938

Chelsea House Publishers
1974 Sproul Road, Suite 400
Broomall, PA 19008-0914

www.chelseahouse.com

Contributing editor: Cathy Schlund-Vials
Cover design by Takeshi Takahashi
Layout by EJB Publishing Services

Contents

Introduction

HAROLD BLOOM

Snow Falling on Cedars is a kind of amalgam of the prose style of Raymond Carver and the mode of Harper Lee's *To Kill a Mockingbird*. Like Harper Lee's novel, Guterson's combines courtroom drama and the sorrows of an oppressed minority, with the Puget Sound setting near Seattle, Washington, taking the place of Harper Lee's South. Lee's African Americans are replaced by Guterson's Japanese Americans. Both narratives are the best kind of humane Period Pieces: liberal, warmly felt, and lucidly told in clear styles. I am not persuaded that either is a permanent achievement, but each is an exemplary defense of human rights in an America where such rights continue to be thwarted, since I can imagine a third novel in this sequence that will deal with Arab-Americans under suspicion in our Age of Terror.

Guterson's achievement, limited but poignant, is best evaluated by Jane Mendelsohn (in one of the Critical Views reprinted in this *Guide*), who praises the complexity of Hatsue's character, while gently indicating the failure of Ishmael as a fictive representation. He is not only less colorful than Melville's Ishmael in *Moby-Dick*, as Jane Mendelsohn notes, but I would venture that Guterson errs in risking the name, Ishmael, since it evokes thoughts of Melville's masterwork, which nothing in *Snow Falling on Cedars* can sustain.

Another literary problem unsolved by Guterson are the irrelevant echoes of Hemingway that are scattered through the novel. Raymond Carver never surmounted Hemingway's influence on his prose, and perhaps it is inevitable that the ghost of Hemingway lingers in the dialogue composed by Carver's disciple.

The five closing paragraphs of *Snow Falling on Cedars* embody both the virtue and the limitations of the novel:

The wall of water moved on. It traveled a half mile speedily and then gathered beneath the *Islander* so that Kabuo felt it, too. It traveled with nothing more to interrupt it and broke against the shore of Lanheedron Island just before two o'clock in the morning. The whistle of the freighter and the lighthouse diaphone sounded again in the fog. Kabuo Miyamoto, his net set, his radio off, the fog as palpable as cotton around him, replaced the line he'd left on Carl's boat with a reserve he kept stowed in his galley. Perhaps he'd squatted for a moment, building a bowline into the manila, and heard the steam whistle of the passing freighter sounding low across the water. It would have been as sorrowful a sound in that heavy fog as anyone could readily conjure or imagine, and as it grew louder—as the freighter drew closer—it would have sounded all the more forlorn. The freighter passed to the north still blowing, and Kabuo listened to it. Perhaps in that moment he remembered how his father had buried everything Japanese beneath the soil of his farm. Or perhaps he thought of Hatsue and of his children and the strawberry farm he would one day pass to them.

The steam whistle from the freighter faded eastward. It sounded at intervals with the fog whistle from the lighthouse, a higher note, more desolate. The fog closed in, muffling it, and the freighter's note went deep enough so that it seemed otherworldly, not a steam whistle but a cacophony of bass notes rising from the bottom of the sea. Finally it merged with the lighthouse signal so that the two of them sounded at the same moment, a clash of sound, discordant. There was a dissonance, faint, every two minutes across the water, and finally even that disappeared.

Kabuo Miyamoto came home to embrace his wife and to tell her how their lives had changed; the lighthouse dogwatch drew to a close, and Philip Milholland stuffed his notes into a folder and threw himself into sleep. He and the radioman, Robert Miller, slept steadily into the afternoon. Then they awoke and left San Piedro Island, transferred to another station. And Art Moran made his arrest.

Well, thought Ishmael, bending over his typewriter, his fingertips poised just above the keys: the palpitations of Kabuo Miyamoto's heart were unknowable finally. And Hatsue's heard wasn't knowable either, nor was Carl Heine's. The heart of *any* other, because it had a will, would remain forever mysterious.

Ishmael gave himself to the writing of it, and as he did so he understood this, too: that accident ruled every corner of the universe except the chambers of the human heart.

Rereading this (and the rest of the novel, before it) is a mixed experience, at best. The second of these paragraphs plays at symbolism, hardly fused with its naturalism, a frequent flaw in Carver's stories. With the third paragraph, something like Hemingway's plain style is attempted, but barely attained. The staccato distinctiveness of the sentences suggests Hemingway parodying Hemingway.

The fourth and fifth paragraphs are confused in their thinking. Does the heart's will exclude accident? Are our deepest desires so over-determined that character becomes fate? Sigmund Freud thought so, and wanted to believe that there are no accidents, but as a wise sage he knew better. Shakespeare, far wiser, created Hamlet, who understood the truth of our condition, and died of the truth. The Player-King in Hamlet's *The Mousetrap*, the prince's revision of *The Murder of Gonzago*, ends his great speech with a dark wisdom that Guterson might ponder:

Our wills and fates do so contrary run
That our devices still are overthrown,
Our thoughts are ours, their ends none of our own.

Biographical Sketch

For Washingtonian native David Guterson, courtroom dramas and breathtaking Pacific Northwest landscapes were integral parts of a childhood spent observing the details that would later shape his most well-known work to date, *Snow Falling on Cedars*. Born in Seattle on May 4, 1956 to Murray and Shirley Guterson, David was the third of five children. As a youth, Guterson would spend hours exploring the nearby Columbia River Basin, where he passed the time fishing, bird hunting, and hiking. His father Murray, who would eventually become the model for Nels Gudmundsson, the defense lawyer in *Snow Falling On Cedars*, was a distinguished and well-respected criminal defense lawyer in the Seattle area. As a child, Guterson often sat in on his father's trials, which sparked his later interest in both the law and ethical issues. However, Guterson did not want to follow his father's career path. As he asserted in an interview with Elisabeth Sherwin, "In the late 1960s when I was growing up I wanted to be a crusader [like my father] but I didn't want to wear a suit and commute."

The outlet for this desire for justice would come much later in 1974, when Guterson began his collegiate career at the University of Washington. Though not a strong student for most of his elementary and secondary education, Guterson flourished in college. There he was exposed to the writings of Russian authors like Tolstoy, Dostoyevsky, Chekhov, and Turgenev, and another Pacific Northwestern writer, Raymond Carver. It was these authors that Guterson would credit, in a *Publishers Weekly* interview with John Blades, as powerful influences in his literary work. After taking a creative writing class, Guterson made the decision to pursue a writing career. When Guterson was 21 years old, he began to write his own stories and submit them to small magazines. This marked the start of a period Guterson labels as one of "intense derivation," and his work was heavily influenced by Carver's style. Though he received several rejections, he would eventually get published in literary magazines like *Seattle Review*, *Iowa Review*, and *Prairie Schooner*.

After completing his Bachelors of Arts at the University of Washington, Guterson married his high school sweetheart, Robin Ann Radwick, and the couple moved to the East Coast where Guterson enrolled in the creative writing program at Brown University. Guterson soon left the program, citing that it was "too experimental." He returned to Seattle, where he enrolled in the Master of Fine Arts program in Creative Writing at the University of Washington, and he worked with Charles Johnson, the National Book Award-winning author of *The Middle Passage*. Guterson received his M.F.A. in 1982 and continued to write on a part-time basis. He and his wife, along with his four children (Taylor, Henry, Travis, and Angelica) live on Bainbridge Island in Puget Sound, and it is this location upon which the fictional San Piedro Island in *Snow Falling on Cedars* is based. In order to finance his burgeoning writing career, Guterson began teaching English full-time at a local high school in 1984, a position he held until the success of *Snow Falling on Cedars*.

Prior to the publication of *Snow Falling on Cedars* in 1994, Guterson spent his free time writing non-fiction and fiction. In the realm of journalism, Guterson published articles on a variety of subjects that included planned communities, the rights of threatened species, professional sports, American consumerism and home schooling in magazines such as *Sports Illustrated*, *Esquire*, and *Harper's*. After his article on home schooling was published in *Harper's*, he received a commission from Mane Salierno Mason at Harcourt Brace to write a full-length book on the subject. *Family Matters: Why Home Schooling Makes Sense* was published in 1992, and was based on his own experiences home schooling his children. Though critics were quick to point out the fact that Guterson was a public high school teacher advocating home schooling, Guterson maintained that he wanted to counter perceptions of the home schooling movement as one dominated by religious fundamentalists. Guterson eventually became a contributing editor of *Harper's*.

In addition to these non-fictional pursuits, Guterson also continued to send short stories to literary magazines. After

Esquire accepted a story but then elected to not publish it, Guterson culled together ten stories (six that had been published previously, four that had not) into a collection that was published by Harper & Row in 1989. This work, entitled *The Country Ahead of Us, The Country Behind*, represents an intergenerational exploration of masculine identity, self-understanding, and personal relationships. The landscape of the Pacific Northwest figures keenly in the collection, which foreshadows *Snow Falling on Cedars* in both its setting and its preoccupation with the past and its relationship to the present. Though praised by critics, the collection is not widely known, despite a re-issuing of the book after the success of *Snow Falling on Cedars* in 1996.

1999 saw the publication of Guterson's most recent novel, *East of the Mountains*, which chronicles a few days in the life of Dr. Ben Givens, a seventy-three-year-old World War II veteran who has been diagnosed with colon cancer. Like *Snow Falling on Cedars*, *East of the Mountains* includes flashbacks and explores the various impacts of the past on a person's present-day existence. However, unlike its predecessor, *East of the Mountains* is more focused on the individual, and the spiritual journey he explores is quite different from the communal narratives and courtroom dramas found in *Snow Falling on Cedars*. The novel received mixed reviews, and its sales did not match Guterson's previous novel.

Guterson's most recent work, *Our Lady of the Forest* (2003), marks a drastic departure from the historical focus of his previous two novels, reflecting instead contemporary concerns and realities. The protagonist of *Our Lady of the Forest* is Ann Holmes, a sixteen-year-old runaway who sees visions of the Virgin Mary. The novel follows the impact these visions have on the small Pacific Northwestern community of North Fork, Washington, and, in the process, examines the plight of working-class America, the rise of consumerism, and the role of faith in modern society.

The Story Behind the Story

It wasn't until the publication of *Snow Falling on Cedars* in 1994 that David Guterson was able to pursue a full-time writing career. Purchased by Harcourt Brace for $15,000, *Snow Falling on Cedars* was an endeavor that took the author ten years to complete. He spent two years deliberating over plot lines, and eight years more on researching and writing the novel. After two false starts and the deletion of more than 300 pages of text, Guterson settled on the structure of the work. Guterson conducted extensive interviews with Japanese Americans who lived in the Seattle area, spent hours of time researching the history of the Japanese/Japanese American internment, and focused his attention specifically on the history of the internment in his home state.

As is the case with his other writings, Guterson's personal experiences impacted the writing of *Snow Falling on Cedars*, a novel that begins in 1954 and traverses the history of the internment and World War II. Guterson modeled his characters after figures in his life. His father, as mentioned previously, served as the inspiration for the defense attorney in *Snow Falling on Cedars*, and Ishamael's father, Arthur Chambers, was based on Walt Woodward, the editor of the local paper who took a public stance against the internment. While an English teacher, Guterson taught Harper Lee's *To Kill A Mockingbird*, a novel he credits as one that heavily influenced the organization and the thematic focus found in *Snow Falling on Cedars*. According to Guterson, "I read [the novel] twenty times in ten years and it never got old, only richer, deeper, and more interesting.... I took that structure ... of 2 separate stories that become one ... and used it."

The novel's success far surpassed Guterson's expectations, and the novel sold an impressive 80,000 copies in hardcover, a rare accomplishment for a first-time novelist. However, it was the paperback edition of the novel that catapulted both the work and the author to celebrity status—2.5 million copies were sold following its release in this format. *Snow Falling on*

Cedars spent weeks on the *New York Times* Bestseller List, and has been translated into 24 languages. Guterson received the PEN/Faulkner Award in 1995, and was named in *People* magazine's "50 Most Beautiful People in the World" the following year. That same year, the novel received numerous honors, including the 1996 American Booksellers Book of the Year Award. In 1999, the novel made the leap from page to cinematic stage in the movie version of *Snow Falling on Cedars*, which starred Ethan Hawke and Max Von Sydow. Though he did not write the script, Guterson did consult with the director, Scott Hicks, and has a co-producer credit. The movie was not well received by audiences, though critics did laud the film's scenic attributes.

Works Cited

Blades, John. "David Guterson: Stoic of the Pacific Northwest." *Publishers Weekly*, 5 April 1999: 215.

Sherwin, Elisabeth. "New Author Thanks Harper Lee for Leading the Way." *Printed Matter*, 12 November 1995.

List of Characters

Ishmael Chambers is the 31-year-old protagonist of the novel. He is the editor of the local paper, the *San Piedro Review*, a position he inherited from his father Arthur Chambers. He is initially introduced as a reporter covering the trial of Carl Heine Jr's accused murderer, Kabuo Miyamoto. A World War II veteran, Ishmael was wounded at the Battle of Tarawa, an injury that left him with one arm. A native of San Piedro, Ishmael grew up with Hatsue Miyamoto (Imada), with whom he shared an intimate relationship. Resentful and bitter because of his wartime experiences and the dissolution of his relationship with Hatsue, Ishmael undergoes an individual journey that eventually leads to a reconciliation of the past and the acceptance of the present. It is Ishmael who holds the key to proving Kabuo's innocence, and his decision to reveal the truth behind Carl Heine Jr.'s death at the conclusion of the novel marks the culmination of this journey.

Hatsue Miyamoto (Imada) is the wife of Kabuo Miyamoto. She and Ishmael Chambers were childhood friends who had a romantic relationship in adolescence. As the novel progresses, it becomes apparent that Hatsue's life has been shaped by two contradictory worlds. Hatsue is compelled by her sense of familial duty to adhere to a traditional Japanese cultural expectation. However, her relationship with Ishmael Chambers represents a desire to embrace a more individual, nontraditional societal role. She and her family are relocated to Manzanar, and it is at this point that Hatsue recognizes the political realities of racism and prejudice. After Hatsue's mother Fujiko confronts her about Ishmael's love letters, Hatsue reconsiders her relationship with Ishmael, realizing that she is not in love with him. She decides to end the relationship with Ishmael, and this rejection, along with his experiences in World War II, are presented as the root causes of Ishmael's bitterness and resentment.

Kabuo Miyamoto is a second generation Japanese American who is on trial for the murder of Carl Heine Jr. A World War II veteran, Kabuo is haunted by the memories of killing German soldiers in battle. His classmates included Carl Heine Jr. and Hatsue Imada. Married to Hatsue, Kabuo has spent the time after the war consumed with the desire to own the land his father had purchased from Carl Heine Sr., which was lost after Etta Heine sold the seven acres to Ole Jurgensen. Trained in the art of kendo (Japanese stick fighting), Kabuo becomes the prime suspect in Carl Heine Jr.'s murder after the assessment made by the coroner, Horace Whaley, who asserts that the mark found on Carl's skull resembles mortal wounds inflicted by Japanese soldiers.

Carl Heine Jr., a career fisherman, is the son of Etta and Carl Heine and Susan Marie's husband. It is his death that opens the novel. Classmate of Kabuo, Ishmael, and Hatsue, Carl Jr. serves as a link between the three major characters both figuratively and literally. Like Kabuo and Ishmael, Carl is a World War II veteran. He is described as a physically robust man who is emotionally distant and a loner as a result of the war. As a child, he and Kabuo were friends, yet as a result of the internment and the war, their friendship has dissolved. It is Carl Jr. who buys Ole Jurgensen's land (which was originally contracted to Zenhichi Miyamoto), and this purchase precipitates a meeting with Kabuo.

Art Moran is the local San Piedro sheriff who investigates Carl Heine Jr's death.

Abel Martinson is Art Moran's young, inexperienced deputy.

Horace Whaley is the local coroner and a World War II veteran. During the war, Horace served as a wartime doctor, and he has been traumatized as a result of his experiences. It is Horace who makes the remark about Carl's head injury, which reminds him of mortal wounds inflicted by Japanese soldiers.

Judge Llewellyn Fielding presides over Kabuo Miyamoto's murder trial.

Ed Soames is the court bailiff in Kabuo Miyamoto's murder trial.

Alvin Hooks is the prosecuting attorney in Kabuo Miyamoto's murder trial. He has charged Kabuo with first-degree murder and is seeking the death penalty. Throughout the trial, Alvin subtly appeals to racial stereotypes about Japanese and Japanese Americans.

Nels Gudmundsson is the defense attorney for Kabuo Miyamoto. Blind in one eye, Nels is recognized by the San Piedro community as an upstanding, intelligent attorney. In his closing arguments, Nels urges the jury to go beyond race and stereotype in their deliberations.

Ole Jurgensen is a white farmer in San Piedro. After Carl Heine Sr.'s death, Etta Heine violated her husband's contract and sold Zenhichi Miyamoto's seven acres to Ole. In 1954, Ole has a stroke and, unable to continue farming, puts his farm up for sale. Carl Heine Jr. quickly buys the land, prompting Kabuo Miyamoto to ask him to consider selling the land to him.

Dr. Sterling Whitman is a hematologist from the mainland town of Anacortes. A witness for the prosecution, Dr. Whitman testifies about the blood found on the fishing gaff, which is assumed to be the murder weapon.

Army Sgt. Victor Maples is one of the witnesses for the prosecution in Kabuo Miyamoto's murder trial. Stationed at the Manzanar internment camp, Army Sgt. Maples testifies to the fact that Kabuo was a highly skilled kendo practitioner.

Arthur Chambers is Ishamel Chambers's father. As founder and editor of *San Piedro Review*, Arthur was an established presence in the community. During the war and in the face of controversy, Arthur used his editorial column to speak out against the internment, emphasizing that the forced relocation of Japanese and Japanese Americans was racist in scope.

Helen Chambers is Ishmael Chambers's mother and the widow of Arthur Chambers. She is concerned about Ishmael's solitary nature, and she urges him to learn to forget the past and live in the present. Like her husband, she is committed to tolerance and honesty.

Carl Heine Sr. is Carl Heine Jr.'s father. Owner of a large strawberry farm, Carl Sr. elects to sell Zenhichi Miyamoto seven acres. It is Carl Sr. who establishes a contract payment system with Zenhichi, and, when Zenihichi and his family are forced to relocate to an internment camp, Carl Sr. promises to keep the contract. Carl Sr. dies soon after the war begins, and his wife, Etta Heine, nullifies the contract and sells the land to a white farmer, Ole Jurgensen.

Etta Heine is the mother of Carl Heine Jr. and the widowed wife of Carl Heine Sr. Bitterly racist and anti-Japanese, Etta is incensed by her husband's decision to sell the seven acres of land to Zenhichi Miyamoto. After her husband's death, Etta sells the land to a white farmer, Ole Jurgensen. It is this sale that serves an important function in the plot, for it provides Kabuo (according to prosecutor Alvin Hooks) with a possible motive for murder.

Susan Marie Heine is Carl Heine Jr's widow. She is described as attractive, sensual, and blond. After Carl's death, Susan reevaluates their marriage, coming to the conclusion that the primary foundation to their relationship was sexual in scope.

Fujiko Imada is Hatsue Miyamoto's mother. A first generation Japanese immigrant, Fujiko represents the traditional aspects of Japanese culture. Distrustful of white Americans, who she refers to as *hakiyin*, Fujiko urges her daughters to follow Japanese customs and gender roles. The Imada family is relocated to Manzanar, following the bombing of Pearl Harbor. While in the camp, Fujiko finds love letters written by Ishmael to Hatsue. Fujiko encourages Hatsue to end her relationship with Ishmael. After her mother's prompting, Hatsue comes to the conclusion that she can never love Ishmael, and she ends the relationship.

Mrs. Shigemura is a first generation Japanese woman who is a representative of traditional Japanese culture. When Hatsue is 13, she is sent to Mrs. Shigemura, who trains her in Japanese social graces. Mrs. Shigemura tells Hatsue to avoid white men, who tend to fetishize Japanese and Japanese American women. She also encourages Hatsue to marry a Japanese man.

Josiah Gillanders is the president of the San Piedro Gill-Netters Association. Called by the defense, he testifies that gill-netters only board each other's boats in cases of emergency. This undermines the prosecution's assertion that Kabuo Miyamoto forcibly boarded Carl Heine Jr.'s boat. His testimony helps establish an alternate version of events the night Carl Heine Jr. was murdered.

Alexander Van Ness is a local boat builder and member of the jury in Kabuo Miyamoto's trial. He does not believe the evidence presented in the case proves Kabuo's guilt beyond a reasonable doubt, and refuses to convict and render a guilty verdict.

Summary and Analysis

Snow Falling on Cedars opens on December 6, 1954 with a court scene, and the reader is immediately introduced to one of the principal characters in the novel—Kabuo Miyamoto. Kabuo is described in physical terms; his dress, his stature, and his demeanor are detailed in the first paragraph of the novel. According to the omniscient unidentified narrator, "Kabuo's features were smooth and angular ... in the face of the charge that had been leveled against him he sat with his dark eyes trained straight ahead and did not appear moved at all" (1). This description anticipates later discussions of Kabuo's "innocence" vis-à-vis the crime for which he stands trial. More specifically, he has been charged with the murder of Carl Heine Jr. and faces the death penalty. Kabuo's stoic and proud manner during the proceedings reflects his demeanor within the larger community of San Piedro Island. This fictional place is, according to the narrator, located in the Puget Sound region of Washington, close to Seattle. Additionally, this initial description establishes Kabuo as a figure marked by a silence, and this silence is the first of many introduced and explored in *Snow Falling on Cedars*.

Chapter 1 also introduces the reader to the other primary and secondary characters in the novel. Written from a third person omniscient perspective, the narrative voice in this first chapter reflects a reporter's sensibility in both its detachment and its attention to detail. Interestingly, the narrator's voice echoes the profession of the protagonist Ishmael Chambers, though it is important to note that Ishmael is not the main narrator of the story. Ishmael is described as "the local reporter ... a man of thirty-one with a hardened face, a tall man with the eyes of a war veteran. He had only one arm, the left having been amputated ten inches below the shoulder" (7). The details included in this description reveal Ishmael's present occupation, military past, and personal losses. Ishmael also acknowledges that he knew the accused prior to the trial—the two had attended the same high school. Chapter 1 also introduces the reader to another key figure, Hatsue Miyamoto, the "accused man's wife" (8).

Ishmael attempts to talk to Hatsue in this opening scene; she tells him to "go away." This interaction is one of the most significant moments in the Chapter 1, for it hints at a past relationship between the two characters, and the exploration of this relationship will provide one of the major plot lines in the novel. It is later revealed that the two grew up in the same community and had a romantic relationship that was complicated by their different ethnic and racial backgrounds, World War II, and the internment. Also included in Chapter 1 are descriptions of other ancillary figures in the novel, from the judge presiding over the case to the members of the jury. In addition to these figures, the name of the victim in the case, Carl Heine Jr., is introduced.

In addition to introducing the major characters, Chapter 1 also introduces San Piedro Island, the setting for *Snow Falling on Cedars*. The snowstorm, which is mentioned repeatedly in this opening chapter, begins as an elemental part of the setting and will, as the novel progresses, accrete more meaning as a metaphor for the historical events that have shaped and overwhelmed the San Piedro community. According to the narrator, "San Piedro was an island of five thousand damp souls" (5) and the reader is provided with a brief history of this Puget Sound locale. The narrator does not reveal the most troubling aspect of San Piedro's history in this introduction—the forced relocation of its Japanese and Japanese American residents (the internment). This, like the relationship between Hatsue and Ishmael, is unveiled in the novel's subsequent chapters, which take the narrative form of flashbacks and memories experienced by both primary characters in *Snow Falling on Cedars* and through the "real time" testimonies of witnesses in Kabuo's murder trial. These flashbacks and testimonies are interspersed throughout the novel.

Chapters 2, 3, and 4 reveal the "facts" upon which the case against Kabuo is based. The first witness called by prosecutor Alvin Hooks is the country sheriff Art Moran, who testifies that Carl Heine's boat, the *Susan Marie*, was found adrift on the morning of September 16, 1954. Through the course of Art's testimony, the narrative shifts into the past, and the details of that particular day are revealed using a present tense. Art's flashback, which is rendered through the voice of the omniscient narrator, is significant in *Snow Falling on Cedars*, for it is a structure that is replicated throughout the novel. Art and his deputy, Abel Martinson, investigate the scene, eventually finding Carl's body trapped underwater in a fishing net. They examine the body, noting that Carl's skull "had been crushed just above his left ear" and that "the bone had fractured and left a dent in his head" (19). This detail, which concludes **Chapter 2**, is revisited in Chapter 5, when the local coroner, Horace Whaley, is called to the stand.

Chapter 3 begins with Nels Gudmundsson, the defense attorney in the case, who is described by the omniscient narrator as a seventy-nine year old man. The description provided focuses on vision; according to the narrator, he was:

> blind in his left eye and could distinguish only shades of light and darkness through its transient, shadowy pupil. The right, however, as to make up for this deficiency, seemed preternaturally observant, even prescient, and as he plodded over the courtroom floorboards, advancing with a limp toward Art Moran, motes of light winked through it. (20)

This description of Nels is significant, for it establishes the defense attorney's attributes. Honest, intelligent, and prescient, Nels consistently stresses the facts of the case, and he calls attention to the issue of anti-Japanese sentiment and its possible impact on the final verdict. Nels, during his cross-examination of Art, questions the sheriff about the items found on Carl's boat. Focusing his questions on the dead engine battery found during the investigation, Nels puts forth the possibility that Carl's death was an accident. More specifically, Nels points out that the battery found was one that was not normally used in Carl's boat. It matches the type of battery Kabuo used on his boat, and an alternate version of the day's events emerges. The prosecution's case is based on the assumption that Kabuo boarded Carl's boat with the intent of murder. However, Kabuo, according to Nels, could have boarded the *Susan Marie* to replace a battery, and that would explain how the battery was found on Carl's boat. Chapter 3 ends with the sheriff's acknowledgment of this possibility.

In **Chapter 4**, Judge Lewellen Fielding calls a brief recess and the narrative focus shifts from the trial to Ishmael Chambers, who reflects on Carl's death. Ishmael has known Carl since childhood, and the first part of the chapter is spent recounting Ishmael's youth. Both Carl and Ishmael graduated in 1942, and though it is not mentioned in this part of the narrative, this is the same year that witnessed the mass relocation of Japanese and Japanese Americans who lived on the West Coast to internment camps. Ishmael also remembers that he and Carl played football, and he briefly recalls a conversation the two shared before a game in November 1941, weeks before the bombing of Pearl Harbor on December 7th. Incidentally, Kabuo's trial takes place in the first week of December, which includes the anniversary of Pearl Harbor. This coincidence is thematically and structurally important—as the novel progresses, it becomes apparent that Kabuo's trial is, in many ways, a re-enactment of those moments following the bombing of Pearl Harbor. After this attack, Japanese and Japanese American residents were considered "traitors" to the United States government by the nation at large were imprisoned. As the events of Chapters 5, 6, and 7 reveal, Kabuo's alleged guilt is partially attributed to his Japanese ancestry, and the sociopolitical realities of the United States before and after World War II are explored in fictionalized form in the novel's plot and thematic focus.

Continuing in this exploration of Chapter 4, the mention of these dates is significant given the historical focus of *Snow Falling on Cedars*; more specifically, the author provides these date clues initially without a larger historical context, instead focusing on the individual significance in the protagonist's life. Absent from these passages are explanations about the larger national and global picture—for example, Pearl Harbor, the entrance of the United States into World War II, and the internment. However, these larger historical events are in the background of Ishmael's personal remembrances, setting the stage for similar explorations of the impact of history on the lives of individuals. As the novel progresses, the significance of these dates becomes more apparent as the protagonist remembers the events that dramatically affected his relationship with Hatsue.

Chapter 4 continues with Ishmael's personal reflections, which include mentions of the loss of his arm in World War II, his experiences attending college in Seattle, and his decision to return to San Piedro to work at his father's newspaper, the *San Piedro Review*. Arthur Chambers, who is introduced in this chapter, is revealed through Ishmael's remembrances, and the reader finds out that Arthur founded the paper after working in the logging industry and serving as a soldier in World War I. Ishmael also muses on his experiences reading *Moby Dick*, which bears a famous literary predecessor to his name in the form of the narrator, who opens the text with the lines, "Call me Ishmael." The narrative then shifts to the day following Carl's death, providing further details about Art Moran's investigation. Ishmael, in the role of a reporter, follows the investigation, which the sheriff initially asserts is not a murder. The chapter concludes with Ishmael's promise to Art that he will not characterize the death as a murder in his paper, and the sheriff agrees to keep Ishmael apprised of any new developments in the case.

Thus, as evidenced by Chapter 4, it is through a flashback structure that other details about San Piedro emerge. The character of the island is revealed through interactions had with the local fisherman, who "learned to be silent" (39). This silence is emblematic of the community of San Piedro, the members of which do not talk openly about the intense racism and prejudice which were integral to the relocation of its Japanese and Japanese American residents. This flashback also provides a further insight into the character of those who inhabit this isolated island community.

Chapter 5 opens with Horace Whaley's testimony. Horace is both the local coroner and a practicing physician, and the reader learns that he served as a doctor in World War II. During Horace's testimony, the narrative time travels from the present-day atmosphere of the courtroom to the initial examination of Carl's body. Two important observations are revealed in Horace's flashback. First, in removing Carl's clothes, Horace finds a watch, which has stopped at one forty-seven. This "clue" is, given the novel's conclusion, significant, for it is eventually used to prove Kabuo's innocence. Second, Horace notices the wound on Carl's skull. According to the narrator:

> Whatever had caused this wound—a narrow, flat object about two inches wide—had left its telltale outline behind the deceased man's head. It was precisely the sort of lethal impression Horace had seen at least two dozen times in the Pacific war, the result of close-in combat, hand to hand, and made by a powerfully wielded gun butt. The Japanese field soldier, trained in the art of *kendo*, or stick fighting, was exceptionally proficient at killing in this manner. And the majority of Japs, Horace recalled, inflicted death over the left ear, swinging in from the right. (55–56)

The above passage reflects the internal thoughts of the coroner, and these observations are soon made public in a conversation between Horace and the county sheriff. It is the revelation of this observation that prompts Art to consider the possibility that Carl was murdered, and provides the sheriff with a possible profile of the culprit. In terms of the plot, this exchange leads the sheriff to suspect that someone of Japanese descent is responsible for the crime. On another level, the coroner's prejudices against the Japanese are vividly illustrated in this moment—he uses, in this reflection, the label "Japs," a term that is racist in its application and reflective of the anti-Japanese sentiment that ran rampant in San Piedro during World War II. And, as is the case with other personal remembrances in the novel, the specter of the past haunts the reality of the present, and the coroner's experiences in the war color his present-day observations. The chapter ends with Horace's assertion that "if he were inclined to play Sherlock Holmes he ought to start looking for a Jap with a bloody gun butt—a right-handed Jap, to be precise" (59).

Chapter 6 begins with Nels Gudmundsson's cross-examination of Horace, who asks the coroner to detail the cause of Carl's death. After a series of questions posed by the defense attorney, Horace acknowledges that Carl must have been breathing when he hit the water, based on the fact that a foamy mix of air, mucus, and seawater had been found in Carl's lungs. Following this revelation, the narrative moves from the coroner's recollections to Art Moran's remembrances. Art recalls the day he broke the news of Carl's death to his wife, Susan Marie. Upon hearing that her husband has died, a shocked Susan Marie whispers to the sheriff, "I knew this would happen one day" (73). The meaning of this statement is unclear to the sheriff, who at the time is taken aback by her statement. However, as the plot unfolds, this statement takes on multiple meanings. On one hand, Susan Marie is referring to the hazards of gill-net fishing and the realities of the profession. On the other hand, given the larger historical framework upon which then novel is set, the statement has added weight and seems to encapsulate the inevitability that the San Piedro community would have to revisit, in a substantive manner, their role in the internment.

In the beginning of **Chapter 7**, the omniscient narrator relates:

> In the back of Judge Lew Fielding's courtroom sat twenty-four islanders of Japanese ancestry, dressed in the clothes they reserved for formal occasions. No law compelled them to take only these rear seats. They had done so instead because San Piedro required it of them without calling it a law. (75)

It is in this chapter that the Japanese and Japanese American members of the San Piedro community are introduced; though

Kabuo and Hatsue are mentioned in the opening pages of the novel, it is in this section that the particular history of this group is examined. Additionally, the first paragraph of Chapter 7 alludes to a history of separation and prejudice in San Piedro, which is explored in more depth as the chapter progresses and sets the stage for the revelations made in Chapters 8 and 9.

Chapter 7 also relates the history of Japanese immigration to the area. The Japanese residents of San Piedro first came to the island in the early 1880s, seeking employment and opportunity in the United States. Most of these immigrants were poor, and they initially found work in the lumber mill in the nearby community of Port Jefferson. According to the omniscient narrator, "in 1907 eighteen Japanese were injured or maimed at the Port Jefferson mill. Jap Number 107, the books indicate, lost his hand to a ripping blade ... Jap Number 57 dislocated his right hip on May 29 ... " (76). As the passage illustrates, racist labels were used to distinguish Japanese immigrants in the workplace, where names are omitted in favor of an impersonal label. On another level, the numbering system used foreshadows the one in place to track Japanese and Japanese American internees, who were catalogued in similar fashion. After the closing of the mill in 1921, San Piedro's Japanese residents shifted to a more agricultural economic base, occupying positions as pickers, sharecroppers, and contract farmers who harvested strawberries and raspberries.

As Chapter 7 continues, the realities of the legal system, which circumscribed the livelihood of Japanese immigrants, are explored alongside mentions of the internment. For example, the omniscient narrator states, "The law said they could not own land unless they became citizens; it also said that they could not become citizens so long as they were Japanese" (76). This narratival assertion alludes to the legal actualities of the first part of the twentieth century. More specifically, laws in states like California, Oregon, and Washington forbade first generation Asian immigrant land ownership, and the federal law prohibited Asian immigrants from obtaining naturalized citizenship.[1] As a consequence of this legislative prohibition, first generation Japanese immigrants often placed land titles in the names of their American-born children, who were considered, under the law, citizens of the United States. In San Piedro, some farmers, like Kabuo's father Zenhichi, orchestrated informal purchase agreements with white landowners like Carl Heine Sr. The recounting of this agreement occurs primarily in Chapter 9, when Etta Heine, the mother of the deceased and the wife of Carl Heine Sr., takes the stand.

As mentioned previously, Chapter 7 also provides the reader with the first explicit mention of the internment. According to the narrator:

> Early on the morning of March 29, 1942, fifteen transports of the U.S. War Relocation Authority took all of San Piedro's Japanese Americans to the ferry terminal in Amity Harbor.... They were loaded onto a ship while their white neighbors looked on, people who had risen early to stand in the cold and watch this exorcising of the Japanese from their midst—friends, some of them, but the merely curious, mainly, and fisherman who stood on the decks of their boats out in Amity Harbor. The fisherman felt, like most islanders, that this exiling of the Japanese was the right thing to do, and leaned against the cabins of their stern-pickers and bow-pickers with the conviction that the Japanese must go for reasons that made sense: there was a war on and that changed everything. (79)

This description follows the pattern of historical revelation that has occurred in previous chapters. The reader is given a precise date for the internment, along with the reactions of San Piedro's non-Japanese / Japanese American residents. Though fictional in scope, the above passage reflects the larger history that envelops the novel—San Piedro is representative of other West Coast communities that were, for the most part, complicit in the evacuation of its Japanese residents. Moreover, the communal history of San Piedro's Japanese and Japanese American residents that is provided in

Chapter 7 shifts to a more personal, individualized account through the remembrances of Hatsue, one of "San Piedro's Japanese Americans" who was forcibly relocated to an internment camp.

This shift from a communal to a personal history occurs through the description of the annual Strawberry Festival, one of the few places where all the residents of San Piedro (those of Japanese descent and their white counterparts) interacted outside the confines of the workplace. Hatsue becomes a dominant figure in this chapter. She is mentioned briefly as the winner of the annual Strawberry Festival beauty pageant, where she is named the "strawberry princess." In the same chapter, Hatsue's familial history is revealed—her father, Hisao Imada, is a first generation Japanese immigrant who has worked as a mill hand and as a small farmer. Her mother, Fujiko, had immigrated to the United States to marry Hisao as part of an arranged marriage orchestrated by a professional matchmaker (*baishakunin*). The professional matchmaker has misrepresented Hisao's wealth to Fujiko and her family, and Fujiko is under the impression that she is marrying a wealthy man. Upon arriving in the United States, Fujiko realizes that Hisao is quite poor, and though initially resentful, she chooses to remain in the United States and works with her husband in the fields.

The past is momentarily interrupted by the present, when Hatsue asks the deputy sheriff, Abel Martinson, for a private meeting with her husband. Abel refuses to grant Hatsue's wish, and the narrative shifts to Hatsue's personal remembrances of her adolescence, which include her sessions with Mrs. Shigemura, a Japanese teacher of social graces who warns 13-year-old Hatsue to avoid white men. Also included are descriptions of Hatsue's young adult life in an internment camp and her subsequent marriage to Kabuo, who, despite Hatsue's protestations, leaves the camp to serve as an Army soldier in World War II. As is the case in previous chapters, Chapter 7 connects the fictional realm of San Peidro with the realties of U.S. history, and the experiences of the island's Japanese residents reflect contemporary issues facing Asian immigrants in the years before and during World War II. Hatsue's remembrances serve as personalized accounts of events that impacted over 110,000 Japanese and Japanese Americans. Kabuo's decision to enter the war also points to a historical actuality—the enlistment of thousands of Japanese American men into the Armed Forces during the period of the internment.[2]

Ishmael's remembrances serve as the focus of **Chapter 8**, which reveals, in more detail, the history of his relationship with Hatsue. The two were childhood friends, and it was with Hatsue that Ishmael experienced his first kiss. Their relationship takes on a more romantic nature in adolescence, after Ishmael sees Hatsue picking strawberries. They kiss for a second time, and ten days pass before they meet again. During this time, Ishmael hides in the forest in front of Hatsue's house, hoping to catch a glimpse of her. Eventually, Ishmael and Hatsue do meet again, and this meeting takes place in a hollowed-out cedar tree in the forest. This place figures keenly in the novel, for it provides Ishmael and Hatsue a refuge from societal constraints and prejudices.

It is in Chapter 8 that some of the problems associated with Ishamel and Hatsue's relationship are explored, and the two have a conversation about these difficulties. Because of the prevailing prejudices of the both the white and Japanese / Japanese American communities, Hatsue and Ishmael decide to conduct their relationship in secret. Ishmael maintains that the interracial aspect of their meetings "doesn't matter" (112), despite Hatsue's remarks about their racial and cultural differences. The chapter ends with a description of this first meeting in the cedar tree, and the omniscient narrator relates:

> With the rain falling outside and the moss softly under him Ishmael shut his eyes and breathed the smell of her [Hatsue] fully in through his nostrils. He told himself he had never felt so happy, and he felt a sort of ache that this was happening and would never again happen in this way no matter how long he lived. (112)

This concluding moment is significant, for it establishes one of the reasons behind Ishmael's bitterness. As subsequent chapters reveal, it is the dissolution of this relationship, the historical events that circumscribed it, and the loss of innocence it brings, that has haunted Ishmael, who cannot seem, for most of the novel, to move past these adolescent remembrances.

Chapter 9 brings the reader back to the courtroom setting when Etta Heine takes the stand. The scene begins with an examination of the witness by the prosecutor. Etta, a German immigrant who met her husband Carl in North Dakota, recounts the agreement her husband shared with Zenhichi Miyamoto. Throughout her testimony, Etta stresses that she advised her husband not to enter into this agreement with Zenhichi, who she doesn't trust because he is Japanese. Her anti-Japanese sentiment is apparent in a flashback moment involving a disagreement with Carl Sr. over his decision to sell Zenhichi seven acres of land; Etta tells her husband, "We're not such paupers as to sell to Japs, are we?" (119). The specifics of the sale—the cost of the land, coupled with the payment agreement between Carl Sr. and Zenhichi—are also revealed in Chapter 9. The narrative shifts to 1942, after Zenhichi receives notification that he and his family will have to evacuate San Piedro. Zenhichi, who is only two payments away from owning the land, talks to Carl Sr. about the contract, which he fears will be lost because the internment. Carl Sr. promises to keep the contract.

The contract details are further enumerated in **Chapter 10**, in which Etta discusses, in her testimony, her decision to nullify the contract following her husband's death in 1944. She returns the money Zenhichi has paid up to the point of the internment, and sells the seven acres to a white framer, Ole Jurgensen. After Kabuo returns from the war, he visits the Heine home, and it is through an exchange with Etta that he realizes that she has sold the land and has no intention of honoring the previous contract. The two argue, and Etta testifies that she felt threatened by Kabuo and had asked her son, Carl, to watch him carefully. This disagreement over land, according to the prosecutor, is further evidence of

Kabuo's motive in murdering Carl Jr. During cross-examination, Nels emphasizes that Etta, in selling her land to Ole at a higher price than what Zenhichi had originally agreed to pay, has profited financially from the exchange. The chapter ends with Ole Jurgensen, who testifies that following a stroke in June 1954 he decided to sell the disputed seven acres. Kabuo had inquired about the land the same day, but was told that Carl Jr. had already given him a down payment, and the prosecutor uses this information as further evidence of the defendant's motive. Chapters 9 and 10 are significant to *Snow Falling on Cedars*'s plot in that they reveal the connections between the defendant and the deceased. Thematically, these disagreements take on more weight given the history of Japanese/Japanese American and white relations in San Piedro and the impact World War II had on the domestic front in West Coast communities.

Chapter 11 provides the reader with the first focused account of the trial from the perspective of the accused. The section begins in Kabuo's cell, which bears a strong resemblance to the description provided of the internment camp barracks in both its austerity and coldness. Kabuo reflects on the events of the past, centering on his interactions with Hatsue and his decision to enlist in the Army. Kabuo also recounts his experiences in battle, reliving in vivid detail the moment he killed a German soldier. His experiences in war, which mirror those had by the other World War II veterans in the novel (Ishmael, Carl Jr., and Horace Whaley) have changed him considerably. Kabuo's reflections of war, however, illustrate the extent to which his silent, stoic demeanor in the courtroom is an effect of his guilt over the killing of German soldiers in the war. As the omniscient narrator observes:

> The face in the hand mirror was none other than the face he [Kabuo] had worn since the war had caused it—because this face was a burden to wear—it remained his, unalterable finally. He knew himself privately to be guilty of murder, to have murdered men in the course of war, and it was this guilt—he knew no other word—that lived

in him perpetually and that he exerted himself not to communicate. (155)

Kabuo continues to remember, recounting his relationship with Hatsue, whom he had known as a teenager and had married while the two of them were interned in the camp. He recalls the moment that Hatsue confronted him about his decision to enlist. And, Kabuo's memories take him back to his childhood, when he began his *kendo* training with his father. By the age of sixteen, Kabuo had mastered the art, and no one in San Piedro could defeat him. The chapter concludes with Kabuo's meditation on his "dark ferocity" (168), which he attributes to his samurai warrior lineage. It is this "dark ferocity" that Kabuo explores in his recollections about the war, and he characterizes his present-day imprisonment not as a consequence of Carl Jr.'s death but as a just punishment for "the lives he had taken in anger" (169) during the war.

Chapter 12 begins with a description of the storm, which "had settled on the town" leaving:

a snow so ethereal it could hardly be said to have settled at all; instead it swirled like some icy fog, like the breath of ghosts, up and town Amity Harbor's streets ... one's field of vision narrowed in close, went blurry and snowbound, fuzzy and opaque, the sharp scent of frost burned in the nostrils of those who ventured out of doors ... When they looked out at the whiteness of the world the wind flung it sharply at their narrowed eyes and foreshortened their view of everything. (170)

The snowstorm, a constant presence throughout the narrative, is used in the above passage, mirrors the plot and serves as a lens upon which to consider the revelations that occur through the course of the novel. More specifically, throughout the trial, the treatment of the past resembles the characteristics of the storm, causing those in the courtroom to "narrow their eyes" and closely examine the world through a "foreshortened view." Simultaneously, the whiteness of the storm becomes, in certain moments of the novel, a reflection of some of the white characters in the novel, who are narrow-minded in both their vision of the past and their views of Japanese and Japanese Americans.

The narrative shifts from this description of the storm to Ishamel, who is "walking aimlessly in the snow, admiring it and remembering" (170). Ishmael's memories center on his relationship with Hatsue, their experiences in the hollow cedar tree, the Strawberry Festival of 1941, and the intensification of his feelings for her. They have continued to conduct their relationship in secret, though Ishmael entertains thoughts of marrying her after the two of them graduate. The two discuss their relationship, and Hatsue tells him what Mrs. Shigemura has told her. Mrs. Shigemura's assertion that Hatsue should "marry a boy of her own kind, a Japanese boy from a good family" (175), which also reflects her mother's position, prompts Hatsue to doubt the longevity of her relationship with Ishmael. She tells him that "This can't go on" (175). Ishmael agrees, and when Hatsue asks what they will do, Ishmael replies that he doesn't know.

The specter of the war is a key figure in Chapter 12, and the approach of the war is signaled by Hatsue's mention of an island rumor that a German submarine has been sighted in the harbor, which prompts Ishmael to mention the fact that he will probably be drafted. The scene ends ironically, with the omniscient narrator's assertion that, in these weeks before the bombing of Pearl Harbor, "the war still seemed far away" (176) in the confines of the cedar tree. It is perhaps appropriate, given this staging, that Chapter 13 flashes back to December 1941, just after the Japanese attack on Pearl Harbor.

Chapter 13 follows the reactions of the Japanese and Japanese American community to the news of the attack, which is revealed via word of mouth and newspaper outlets; the Japanese and Japanese American inhabitants of San Piedro are worried about possible retaliations by the government on their community. Ishmael's father, Arthur, confronts this issue and publishes a special war edition of the *San Piedro Review*, which includes information about San Piedro's air-raid safety measures along with an article that maintains that San Piedro's Japanese residents have pledged their loyalty to the United States. This article also mentions that that some Japanese Americans' bank accounts have been frozen as a result of the attack, although the same treatment is not extended to German descendents. The inclusion of this article draws criticism from the community, and some of the white residents choose to cancel subscriptions and write angry letters. However, other residents support Arthur's stance and send him letters that condemn the racial paranoia that has gripped the West Coast.

Hatsue and Ishmael later meet, and Ishmael doesn't initially recognize the possible consequences of the Pearl Harbor attack on Hatsue's family and community. Ishmael asserts that the enemy is Japan, not Japanese Americans, and rationalizes the U.S. entry into the war by stating, "The Japanese *forced* us into it. And on a Sunday morning, when no one was ready. It's cheap, if you ask me, They—" (185). Hatsue interrupts Ishmael and says,

> Look at my face. Look at my eyes, Ishmael. My face is of the people who did it—don't you see what I mean? My face—it's how the Japanese look. My parents came to San Piedro from Japan. My mother and father, they hardly speak English. My family is in bad trouble now. Do you see what I mean? We're going to have trouble. (185)

Hatsue's assertion is prophetic in scope—though Ishmael does not consider Hatsue "Japanese," the distinction between Japanese and Japanese American is one that is overlooked by the larger social order. Ishmael maintains that such world events will not affect their relationship, yet Hatsue continues to assert that they will—and, as the history of the internment and the events of Chapters 14 and 15 illustrate, they have had a profound impact.

On February 4, 1942, two FBI agents arrive at Hatsue's house, and it is this visitation that is recounted in **Chapter 14**. After searching the premises, the two agents confiscate items that are connected to Japanese culture—including a kimono and a bamboo flute. The agents also discover a shotgun and some dynamite Hatsue's father, Hisao Imada, uses to clear fields for strawberry planting. Both possessions are illegal, and Hisao is arrested and relocated to Montana, where he is forced to dig trenches in a work camp. Following the arrest of her husband, Fujiko Imada, Hatsue's mother, tells Hatsue and her sister the story of her journey to the United States, emphasizing the racism and prejudice she experienced from white Americans, who she refers to as *hakujin*. She ends her narrative with a prediction that the family will have to endure more hardship.

It is in Chapter 14 that Hatsue and Ishmael meet for what will be the last time in their relationship. Prior to this final meeting, Hatsue and Ishmael discuss the possible outcomes of the war. Hatsue is worried about the future, while Ishmael maintains that things will work out, and he tells her that he loves her. Hatsue is entrenched in realistic considerations, and it becomes apparent that Ishmael's idealism is naïve, given the events of March 21, 1942, when the U.S. War Relocation Authority orders all Japanese and Japanese American residents on the island to prepare for the internment. Hatsue and Ishmael meet the day before she is supposed to leave for the internment camp. Ishmael devises a plan to communicate with Hatsue by mail. The two share an intimate moment, though "the emptiness she [Hatsue] felt pervaded it and she couldn't put her thoughts away" (212). Hatsue later remembers that it was at this moment of intimacy that she realized that she was not in love with Ishmael. Ishmael asks Hatsue to marry him, but she tells him "no." Hatsue accompanies this refusal with the assertion that she doesn't "want ... [him] ... to be unhappy" and leaves.

The events of **Chapter 15** take place the next morning, and begin with presence of army trucks. These trucks take San Piedro's Japanese and Japanese residents to the Amity Harbor dock, where they begin the first phase of the long journey to Manzanar, an internment camp in the deserts of Southern California. Chapter 15 reveals, through the observations of the omniscient narrator, the conditions in the dusty, crowded camp. Kabuo and Hatsue meet in the camp, and Kabuo works closely with Hatsue's family, taking care of repairs and helping the family with chores. In the meantime, Ishmael's first letter arrives. Hatsue's sister opens the letter and then gives it to her mother. After reading the letter, Fujiko confronts Hatsue, who has already realized that she is not in love with Ishmael. Hatsue replies to Ishmael's letter, ending the relationship. The contents of this letter are revealed in Chapter 24.

Shifting from the Japanese American domestic perspective, **Chapter 16** enumerates Ishmael's war career, which began in "the late summer of 1942" (233). The chapter opens in 1943, while Ishmael is a marine on board the U.S.S. *Heywood*. Ishmael's company is about to storm the island of Betio, part of the Tarawa Atoll in the South Pacific. Loaded in boats before dawn, Ishmael and his fellow marines have been waiting for hours in the waters off Betio. When they finally storm the beach, chaos erupts, and most of Ishmael's company is killed before reaching the shore. Ishmael hides behind a seawall, watching soldiers around him die. When evening arrives, Ishmael and the other remaining troops attempt to storm the beach again, and a bullet hits Ishmael in the left arm. As medics tend to his wound, Ishmael wakens, blacks out, and then wakes again aboard a ship, surrounded by sick and dying soldiers. His arm has been amputated as a result of his injury. Ishmael, under the influence of morphine, refers to Hatsue as the "Jap bitch." Though not explicitly mentioned in Chapter 16, Ishmael's reaction, coupled with the placement of this scene, which occurs after Hatsue's letter has been written and sent, is a possible response to Hatsue's rejection. This rejection, coupled with the horrors experienced in war, has caused Ishmael to lose the idealism he had in adolescence. Like Kabuo, Ishmael's life dramatically changes as a result of the war. The idealism he once had has been replaced by bitterness, an emotional manifestation of Ishmael's inability to reconcile the events of the past.

Back in the courtroom, **Chapter 17** opens with a description of the snowstorm. This snowstorm has wrecked havoc on the San Piedro community, which is shown to be at its mercy. In spite of hazardous driving conditions, the residents of the community venture out to buy necessary supplies to prepare for the blizzard, which, at this point in the narrative, is in full force. The futility of their preparations is revealed in an observation made by the omniscient narrator, who relates:

> ... those who had lived on the island a long time knew that the storm's outcome was beyond their control. The storm might well be like others past that had caused them to suffer, had *killed* even—or perhaps it might dwindle beneath tonight's stars and give their children snowbound happiness. Who knew? Who could predict? If disaster, so be it, they said to themselves. There was nothing that could be done except what could be done. (255)

Interestingly, the above passage thematically and structurally resembles the account of the Battle at Tarawa; the description of the snowstorm, the emphasis on its power, and the outcome of which was "beyond their control" is similar to the circumstances surrounding the storming of the beach. Like the men involved in the battle, the residents of the San Piedro community are at the whim of larger forces. On another level, the description of the storm and the reaction of the long-time residents of the island mirror the events and reactions that encompassed the Japanese and Japanese American community after the bombing of Pearl Harbor. Overwhelmed by the "realities" of war, San Piedro's white residents passively watched as the Japanese and Japanese Americans in their community were relocated to internment camps. This issue of passivity and the consequences of complicity are more fully explored in Kabuo's trial, which figures keenly in Chapters 17–21.

Art Moran is called to the stand, and he describes, in more detail, the circumstances that would eventually lead to Kabuo's arrest. According to the sheriff, one of the mooring ropes found on Carl Jr.'s boat did not match the other three ropes on board; however, it did match the ropes found on Kabuo's ship. Additionally, one of the ropes found on Kabuo's boat is relatively new, which suggested, to the sheriff, that he recently lost one and had to replace it. Art initially came to the conclusion to search Kabuo's boat after conversations with Etta Heine and Ole Jurgensen, who both discussed Kabuo's desire to reclaim his father's land.

Chapter 18 continues with Art Moran's testimony, and the sheriff describes the day that he took Kabuo into custody. The narrative once again shifts to a flashback to this moment, and the narrative is rendered using a present tense construction. After obtaining a warrant from Judge Lewellen Fielding (who, incidentally, is the judge presiding over Kabuo's murder trial), Art and his deputy Abel meet Kabuo at the dock, with the intention to search his boat. Kabuo complies with their request, and the deputy finds a fishing gaff, which has blood on the handle. Kabuo maintains that it is fish blood, and Art interrogates him further, emphasizing the location of the blood on the gaff—it is, according to Art, on the "*butt* end" (268) of the gaff. This detail is significant, for it reveals the impact of Horace Whaley's earlier conversation with the sheriff, when the coroner told the sheriff to "start looking for a Jap with a bloody gun butt—a right-handed Jap, to be precise" (59). The connection between the coroner's assertions and Art's determination of Kabuo's guilt is further strengthened by Art Morgan's internal thoughts, which are revealed by the omniscient narrator. According to the narrator:

> It had occurred to him, too, that for all his arrogance Horace Whaley had been right. For here was the Jap with the bloody gun butt ... here was the Jap he'd been led to inexorably by every islander he'd spoken with.... [he] looked into the Jap's still eyes to see if he could discern the truth there. But they were hard eyes set in a proud, still face, and there was nothing to be read in them either way. They were the eyes of a man with concealed emotions, the eyes of a man hiding something. (269)

It is apparent in the above passage that Art has, in many ways, internalized the racist thoughts of those he has questioned.

Kabuo ceases to be a resident of the island and instead becomes a "Jap," a foreign presence on the island, and, perhaps most significant, a negative stereotype—Kabuo is read by the sheriff as an untrustworthy, inscrutable individual. Though a decade has passed since the internment ended, the perception of untrustworthiness and the essentialized reading of Japanese Americans persists, embodied in the arrest of Kabuo who is, according to Art, guilty by racial and ethnic association. The chapter ends with Art's declaration to Kabuo that he is under arrest.

December 7, 1954 is the date provided in the first sentence of **Chapter 19**, and the narrative returns to the drama in the courtroom. Though the author does not note the significance of the date explicitly, it is important to note that this date marks the anniversary of Pearl Harbor. The chapter begins with the prosecutor, Alvin Hooks, who calls Dr. Sterling Whitman, a hematologist from the mainland town of Anacortes, to the witness stand. Hooks proceeds to ask Dr. Whitman a series of questions about the blood found on the fishing gaff, establishing for both the reader and the jury the fact that it is human blood—type B positive. This matches the blood type of the deceased. The prosecutor also makes a point of emphasizing the rarity of this blood type in white males, and mentions that Kabuo's blood type is O. Thus, according to the prosecutor, the blood found on the gaff is very likely Carl Jr.'s blood, and it is assumed that the fishing gaff was the weapon used in the murder.

Nels Gudmundsson questions Dr. Whitman, and it is under cross-examination that Dr. Whitman admits that no bone splinters, hair, or skin were found on the gaff, which problematizes the notion that the gaff was used to inflict Carl Jr.'s head wound. Dr. Whitman also states that the blood probably came from a minor injury, which matches to the coroner's report that a cut was found on Carl's hand. Moreover, it is revealed that twenty percent of the Japanese population has Kabuo's blood type, which further destabilizes Hooks's assertion that Kabuo was the only person who could have committed the crime.

After a recess, Alvin Hooks brings Army First Sergeant Victor Maples into the courtroom. Sergeant Maples states that he trained Kabuo's regiment, the 442nd which was "composed of Nisei[3] boys" (282), in hand-to-hand combat during World War II. Sergeant Maples recalls Kabuo's expertise in *kendo*, and he maintains with "certainty that the defendant was eminently capable of killing a man larger than himself with a fishing gaff...." Sergeant Maples also alludes to Kabuo's war record, calling him "an excellent soldier" and tells the jury that "it would not surprise [him] to hear that Kabuo Miyamoto had killed a man with a fishing gaff. He was highly capable of such a deed" (285). What is significant in Sergeant Maples's testimony is that though he acknowledges Kabuo's strengths as a solider during World War II, he doesn't make mention of the fact that Kabuo's record reflects his loyalty and dedication to the United States. After all, he did fight in the war as a representative of the United States, despite the fact that his family and community have been unjustly interned.

Chapter 20 marks the conclusion of the prosecutor's case, and the elements of his strategy are enumerated in this section. The last witness called by the prosecution is Susan Marie Heine, the deceased man's wife. According to the omniscient narrator:

> Alvin Hooks ... knew well the value of Susan Marie Heine. He had called to the witness box the county sheriff and the county corner, the murdered man's mother and the bent-over Swede from whom the murdered man had planned to buy his father's old farm. He had proceeded to a variety of secondary witnesses—Sterling Whitman, Dale Middleton, Vance Cope, Leonard George, Sergeant Victor Maples—and now he would finish matters by presenting the wife of the murdered man.... she would persuade [the jury] not precisely with what she had to say but with the entirety of who she was. (287)

This description provides an interesting moment in the novel, for the reader is given an opportunity to assess Alvin Hooks's case thus far. More specifically, the prosecution's case has been built on the testimony of white San Piedro residents and outsiders to the community, and it has, for the most part, been based on circumstantial evidence, speculation, and, perhaps most significant, on stereotype. Most of the witnesses called by the prosecution have, at particular moments in their testimony and in their reflections, made dismissive comments about the Japanese and Japanese Americans. Yet, no Japanese or Japanese American witnesses have been called by the prosecution, which further establishes the racialized undertones in the case. In other words, there are no representatives from Kabuo's community, which remains segregated from their white counterparts in the space of the courtroom (as evident in Chapter 7) and in the larger San Piedro community.

With this in mind, the selection of Susan Marie, who will, according to the prosecutor, sway the jury not for what she says but with "the entirety of who she was," is an important moment of consideration. The omniscient narrator describes Susan Marie as having "the air of an unostentatious young German baroness" (286–287), with blond hair and pale skin. Susan Marie's physical appearance reinforces the sense that she is the embodiment of whiteness. This whiteness, in the space of the courtroom, is juxtaposed with Kabuo's "Japaneseness," which has been established in the testimonies of all the witnesses called by the prosecution.

In her testimony, Susan Marie recounts the day Kabuo, who she repeatedly calls "the Japanese man" (288), visited her husband to discuss the possible sale of the disputed seven acres. The narrative flashes back to this moment, and is rendered in the present tense. Kabuo and Carl go outside to discuss the matter further; while the two men are on the porch, Susan Marie reflects on her courtship with Carl, which was based primarily on a mutual physical attraction. Carl reenters the house, and Susan Marie questions him about the nature of the visit. Carl mentions Kabuo's desire to buy the seven acres, and then discusses, in more detail, the history behind the sale of the land. Carl tells his wife that he is conflicted about selling the land. His mother, after all, is intensely anti-Japanese, and he has mixed feelings about the Japanese and Japanese Americans. Through the course of their discussion, Carl's inability to speak about the past emerges. According to the omniscient narrator,

> Carl had told her more than once—he'd repeated it just the other day—how since the war he couldn't *speak*. Even his old friends were included in this, so that now Carl was a lonely man who understood land and work, boat and sea, his own hands, better than his mouth and heart. (297)

Like Ishmael and Kabuo, a particular silence pervades Carl's post-World War II existence, making him a "lonely man" who is emotionally distant.

However, in spite of this inability to speak, Carl does tell Susan Marie the primary reason for his reluctance to sell the land to Kabuo. Carl states, "It comes down to the fact that Kabuo's a *Jap*. And I don't hate Japs, but I don't like 'em either. It's hard to explain. But he's a Jap" (297). Interestingly, Susan Marie corrects her husband, replying that "He's not a Jap" and reminds him that the two were childhood friends. Carl responds, emphasizing that this relationship was part of the past, "before the war came along" (298). This conversation is interrupted by the cry of one of their children and the discussion ends. Chapter 20 concludes with Susan Marie's memory of the last time she sees Carl before his death, moments before he leaves for the Amity Harbor docks.

Chapter 21 continues with Susan Marie still on the witness stand, and the narrative returns to the present-day trial setting. Nels Gudmunddson questions Susan Marie about her testimony, focusing on whether or not she was present during Carl's conversation with Kabuo. Susan Marie admits, under cross-examination, that she was not physically present during their conversation about the land. Moreover, she eventually concedes that Carl may have led Kabuo to believe that there was a possibility that he would sell the seven acres, for her husband did not tell her that he would not, under any circumstances, consider Kabuo's request. Susan Marie also reveals that Kabuo and Carl were, at one point, close friends, and admits that she cannot speak for her husband, because she does not "know what ...[he] experienced" (306).

This is perhaps the most important part of Susan Marie's testimony, for it is the first time that Nels raises the issue of hearsay and its use in the trial. Returning to the prosecution's strategy, the previous witnesses—from Etta Heine to Sergeant Maples—have based their recollections on speculations about the defendant. After Nels asserts that "There's been a lot of hearsay admitted as evidence," Judge Fielding agrees, replying, "Yes ... A lot of hearsay—hearsay you didn't object to" and tells the jury about the problems of "the Deadman's Statute," which allows those living to speak on behalf of the deceased. Judge Fielding acknowledges that such a statute "creates a ... shady legal area" (306–307) and instructs the jury to take this under consideration. Thus, the prosecution's case is somewhat undermined by this admission, and this occurs ironically through the testimony of Susan Marie, the person who would, as previously mentioned, sway the jury "with the entirety of who she was." Chapter 21 closes with a reintroduction of the storm, which has caused a power outage.

In **Chapter 22**, the trial continues in spite of the power outage, and Alvin Hooks announces that Susan Marie is his last witness and that "the state rests at the same moment the county's power supply does" (308). Judge Fielding calls a recess, and Ishmael goes to his office to pick up his camera to take pictures of the storm for the paper. Ishmael cautiously drives through the streets of San Piedro, stopping to photograph scenes that attest to the destructive nature of the storm—overturned cars, fallen trees, and collapsed power lines. Ishmael then returns to the courthouse, which is still without electricity. Judge Fielding announces that the trial will adjourn the next morning. Ishmael leaves to continue photographing the effects of the storm. In this second outing, Ishmael spots Hatsue and her father on the side of road. Their car is stuck in the snow, and Ishmael offers the two a ride to their house, which they eventually accept. There is an uncomfortable silence in the car, which is broken by Hatsue. Hatsue complains that Kabuo's trial is unfair, and urges

Ishmael to write a column in the *San Piedro Review* defending Kabuo.

Ishmael doesn't tell her that he will write the column, and, as Chapter 22 closes, it is unclear what Ishmael will choose to do. After Hatsue and her father leave the car, Ishmael notes the parallels between the past and the present. According to the omniscient narrator:

> It occurred to him that her husband was going out of her life in the same way he himself once had. There had been circumstances then and there were circumstances then and there were circumstances now; there were things beyond anyone's control. Neither he nor Hatsue had wanted the war to come—neither of them had wanted that intrusion. But now her husband was accused of murder, and that changed things between them. (326)

This moment mirrors the decision that faced Carl Jr. after his meeting with Kabuo, which is recounted by Susan Marie in Chapters 20 and 21. Recognizing the wrongs of the past, both Carl and Ishmael are both haunted by history, which includes the war. Thus, the decision to right the wrongs of the past requires an acknowledgment by both characters of the "circumstances then and ... now," which marks the first step in moving beyond long-held grudges. In the case of Ishmael, his decision whether or not to help Hatsue has important implications, for it will serve as an integral step to Ishmael's development as both a character and as an individual in the novel.

Chapter 23 continues with Ishmael, and he visits the archives at the island's lighthouse to compare the magnitude of the present blizzard to past winter storms. While looking through crates of maritime records, Ishmael's thoughts once again settle on memories of the past, and the narrative shifts to the first time Ishmael saw Hatsue after the war. In this flashback, it is revealed that Ishmael ran into Hatsue in Petersen's, the local grocery store. After noticing Ishmael's arm, Hatsue expresses regret for his injury. Ishmael angrily responds to Hatsue, telling her that "The Japs did it.... They shot my arm off. *Japs*" (332). Though Ishmael later apologizes for the remark, Hatsue remains cold and distant in their subsequent interactions. In this same section of the novel, Ishmael recalls another meeting with Hatsue. Ishmael finds Hatsue alone on the beach, and attempts to have a conversation with her. In this second encounter, Ishmael tells Hatsue that he hasn't been happy since the dissolution of their relationship, and begs her to let him "hold ... [her] once and smell ... [her] hair" (334). Hatsue refuses his request, and maintains that Ishmael must "get up and walk away from here and forget about [her] forever" (334).

These two particular memories reveal the reasons why Ishmael, in Chapter 22, is conflicted about whether or not to help Hatsue. More specifically, as the incident in the grocery store illustrates, Ishmael emphasizes that "the *Japs*" are responsible for his injury, and he includes, by implication, Hatsue in the assignment of blame. In the second memory, Ishmael's desire for Hatsue is still present, in spite of the fact she is married and that, in the grocery store, he conflates her with "the enemy" at the Battle of Tarawa. Thus, the coexistence of two seemingly conflicting senses—love and revenge—has, as the remainder of the novel reveals, shaped Ishmael's existence in the present, and both of these feelings have roots in the past. Though Hatsue tells Ishmael to forget about her and move on with his life, he has, for most of the novel, not been able to follow her advice, and his memories of Hatsue become increasingly bittersweet and couched in the language of loss.

The narrative in Chapter 23 shifts back to the present, when Ishmael finds the maritime records for September 15 and 16, 1954, which include the night of Carl Jr.'s death. In the lighthouse, Ishmael happens upon a clue that will, if revealed, exonerate Kabuo. According to the radio transmission records, a large freighter (the S.S. *West Corona*) radioed for assistance in navigating through the thick fog. The radioman on duty advised the *Corona* to proceed through Ship Channel Bank, where Carl Jr. was fishing that night. According to the records, the freighter passed through the Ship Channel Bank at 1:42 a.m., five minutes before the time found on Carl's watch, which was noted in Horace Whaley's autopsy report. Ishmael pieces together the events and realizes that the freighter would have produced waves large enough to upend Carl's boat and "toss even a big man overboard" (337). Ishmael takes one of the carbon copies of the report. He then asks one of the lighthouse attendants about the whereabouts of the radioman on duty the night of September 15/16. He discovers that the radioman was transferred the next day, which makes Ishmael the only person who knows the truth about Carl Jr.'s death. Chapter 23 concludes with this realization.

In **Chapter 24**, Ishmael visits his mother, Helen Chambers, who is described by the omniscient narrator as "homely and dignified in the manner of Eleanor Roosevelt" (341). The two discuss the details of Kabuo's murder trial. In spite of the fact that Ishmael knows the truth behind Carl Jr.'s death, he tells his mother that he thinks Kabuo is guilty of murder. Helen maintains that the evidence in the case is circumstantial, and asks her son if there are ever enough facts to justify the application of a death sentence. Ishmael admits that his past prejudices have colored his view of the defendant. According to Ishmael:

> None of it [the stereotype of the Japanese as "sly" and "treacherous"] is fair or true, but at the same time I find myself thinking about [these stereotypes] whenever I look at Miyamoto sitting there straight ahead. They [the U.S. government] could have used his face for one of their propaganda films—he's that inscrutable. (345)

Helen counters Ishmael's assertion with a reminder of the similarities between Ishamel and Kabuo. Helen tells her son, "Like you, Ishmael, he served in the war. Have you forgotten that—that he fought in the war? That he risked his life for this country?" (345). Ishmael accepts his mother's point, but maintain that this history has no relevance to the case. Ishmael's statement is ironic given the prosecution's case, which is partially based on the negative stereotypes of the Japanese and Japanese Americans that were formulated in the past.

As Chapter 24 progresses, the discussion between Helen and Ishmael continues. The focus of their conversation moves from the trial to Ishmael's present condition. Helen recognizes that, since the war, her son lives with what she labels a "coldness." Ishmael admits to his mother that he is unhappy, and asks Helen to tell him what to do. Helen responds to her son's inquiry with the assertion that she cannot tell him what to do because she doesn't fully understand what it was like to go to war. Thematically speaking, this exchange between mother and son sets the stage for Ishmael's development as a character; more specifically, as foreshadowed in this conversation, Ishmael's emotional reconciliation must ultimately take place via an individual, personal journey into the past. After this conversation with his mother, Ishmael retreats to his father's study, where he remembers his childhood and his father, Arthur, who died in Seattle at the Veterans Administration Hospital after a bout with cancer. Ishmael recalls his father's reputation as a well-respected part of the San Piedro community, remembering him as a figure that was beloved by both the white and Japanese/Japanese American members in San Piedro Island.

In the concluding pages of Chapter 24, Ishmael rereads the letter Hatsue had sent from Manzanar. Hatsue tells Ishmael that she was not in love with him, and that she realized this during their final meeting, when the two had consummated their relationship. Ishmael replays this moment in his mind, and his memory drifts to the romantic relationships he has since had, which have been short-lived and unfulfilling.

Chapter 24 ends with two important decisions. More specifically, Ishmael elects to not release the information held in the maritime logs, thus hiding the evidence that would, in fact, exonerate Kabuo. Instead, Ishmael decides to write an article defending Kabuo, in order to place Hatsue in his debt. Though Ishmael has, in this section, confronted his past, he is still guided by the wounds of this past in his actions.

Chapter 25 opens on the morning of the third day of the trial, and the case for the defense begins. Hatsue is called by

Nels Gudmundsson to the witness stand. Though outwardly calm, Hatsue is very nervous, and this nervousness prompts a flashback in the narrative. This flashback reveals a moment between Kabuo and Hatsue a few months after the war, after Kabuo has realized that he has lost the claim to his father's land. Hatsue remembers Kabuo's determination in reclaiming the land, and recounts the house her husband spent fishing in order to save enough money to buy it back.

After this revelation, the narrative shifts to the present-day courtroom setting, and Chapter 25 continues with Hatsue's testimony. She testifies that her husband was hopeful that he would recover his family's land following a conversation with Ole Jurgensen, despite the fact that Ole had already accepted a down payment from Carl Jr. According to Hatsue, this optimism increased after Kabuo spoke with Carl Jr. Hatsue, in her testimony, recounts that, on the morning of September 16, Kabuo returned home from fishing "hopeful" (366). He told her that he had come across Carl stranded in his boat and had loaned him a battery. Through the course of the night, the two men talked about the land, and, according to Kabuo, Carl Jr. agreed to sell the seven acres for $8,400. This news is, in Hatsue's testimony, juxtaposed with the events later that same day, when she received a phone call from Jessica Porter, a clerk at Petersen's, who informed her of Carl Jr.'s death.

Chapter 26 begins with Alvin Hooks's cross-examination of Hatsue. It is important to note that the narrative structure in both Chapters 25 and 26 utilize a "real-time" construction, and the past is revealed not through flashback shifts but through accounts told in the past tense. The prosecutor revisits the details of Hatsue's testimony in the previous chapter, and then proceeds to question Hatsue about her and Kabuo's actions following the news of Carl Jr.'s death. Hatsue eventually admits that they chose to keep the details of Kabuo's interaction with Carl Jr. that night from the authorities because they were afraid that this news would be used against Kabuo. According to Hatsue, "Silence seemed better. To come forward seemed like a mistake" (372). Hatsue and Kabuo's fears were, as the trial illustrates, quite founded.

Thematically speaking, this moment in the novel represents another instance of silence. This particular silence is based partially on the strange circumstances of Carl Jr.'s death, but it also comes after Hatsue and Kabuo have both been impacted by the prevailing perceptions of the white San Piedro community. Though Hatsue, prior to the war, has faith that she will not be judged according to her racial background, this attitude shifts as a result of the events that occur immediately after the start of the war—from the internment to Ishmael's anti-Japanese declaration in the grocery store. This silence can be read as the consequence of a history of discrimination, which, as established in previous chapters, is revealed and explored in Kabuo's murder trial.

Hatsue, flustered as a result of Alvin Hooks's cross-examination, is asked by the judge to leave the witness stand. Nels Gudmundsson then calls Josiah Gillanders, the president of the San Piedro Gill-Netters Association, to testify. Josiah testifies that gill-netters board each other's boats only in cases of emergency. This revelation counters the prosecution's assertion that Kabuo may have forcibly boarded Carl Jr.'s boat on the night of his death. Nels Gudmundsson asks Josiah to enumerate the decisions a professional gill-netter would make in an emergency situation, further establishing the implausibility of a forcibly boarding of another fisherman's boat. Nels Gudmundsson concludes his questioning of Josiah, and Alvin Hooks's proceeds with his cross-examination of the witness.

As Chapter 26 continues, Hooks acknowledges the elements of Josiah's testimony, but asks the witness if the defendant could have possibly faked an emergency, which would allowed Kabuo to board Carl Jr.'s boat. This point is significant, given the construction of the prosecution's case thus far. More specifically, Hooks continues to stress, in his cross-examination of both Hatsue and Josiah, Kabuo's untrustworthiness and deceit, which links to previous mentions by other witnesses about the defendant's character, which is often conflated with the stereotype associated with his racial identity. Josiah does concede this point to the prosecution, telling Hooks that "It could have happened.... But I don't much think it did." Chapter 26 concludes as Josiah "left the stand carrying his hat between his fingers" (386).

The opening description in **Chapter 27** reminds the reader of the snowstorm, which "battered the courtroom windows and rattled them in their casements so vigorously it seemed the glass would break" and caused the "citizens in the gallery ... to struggl[e] against it to make their way to and from the courthouse" (387). As in other sections of the novel, this description of the storm reflects the events revealed in the courthouse. More specifically, those in the courtroom have been overwhelmed by the facts of the case. Most significant, the "citizens in the gallery" have been forced to reflect on both the elements of the alleged crime and the history of prejudice and racism that has preceded it. The metaphoric analogy between the storm and the trial is apparent in the omniscient narrator's assertion about the storm's impact. According to the narrator:

> The snow was one thing, falling as it did, but the whine of the storm, the stinging force of it against their faces— everyone wished unconsciously that it would come to an end and grant them peace. They were tired of listening to it. (387)

Though explicitly connected to the storm in the narrative, the above passage can also be taken as a reflection of the trial's impact on those present in the courtroom. After all, the jury has listened to a variety of arguments by both the prosecution and the defense, and the combative nature of the trial echoes the combative nature of the storm. For each of the characters in the novel, the retelling of the events surrounding Carl Jr.'s death have forced them to reflect, vis-à-vis flashbacks and testimonies, the larger historical picture that circumscribes the trial. Taken together, the reader obtains insights on San Piedro as a conflicted community that has, until this trial, not fully taken stock of its past.

With this in mind, Chapter 27 marks a reflective moment in the text. And, it is in this chapter that Kabuo's story dominates.

The other witnesses have testified, in one way or another, to Kabuo's character, his possible motivations, the evidence against him, and his past. Until this moment, the reader and, by proxy the jury, has not been given a full picture of Kabuo's version of events. Though told in a flashback narrative construction, this flashback is told not on the witness stand but in Kabuo's prison cell, and this flashback begins in the days following Kabuo's arrest, when Nels Gudmundsson, who has been assigned to the case, visits the defendant. Nels tells Kabuo that he has reviewed the facts of the case, and asks Kabuo to provide his version of the story. Kabuo initially does not tell Nels Gudmundsson the complete truth—for example, Kabuo denies that he spoke with Carl Jr. the night of his death. Nels, however, does not believe him, and pushes Kabuo to tell him the truth. Kabuo acquiesces, and what follows is a blow-by-blow account of that fateful night's events.

Kabuo, in his conversation with Nels Gudmundsson, reiterates some of the stereotypes that have been explored through the course of the novel. Nels initially tells Kabuo that he understands the reason he lied about his meeting with Carl Jr.; directing his statements to Kabuo, Nels tells him, "You figure because you're from Japanese folks nobody will believe you anyway" (391). Kabuo replies, agreeing with his lawyer, and continues the discussion. According to Kabuo:

> We're sly and treacherous.... You can't trust a Jap, can you? This island's full of strong feelings, Mr. Gudmundsson, people who don't often speak their minds but hate on the inside all the same. They don't buy their berries from our farms, they won't do business with us. You remember when somebody pitched rocks through all the windows at Sumida's greenhouses last summer? Well, now there's a fisherman everybody liked well enough who's dead and drowned in his net. They're going to figure it makes sense a Jap killed him. They're going to want to hang me no matter what the truth is. (391)

Kabuo, in the above passage, points out the various manifestations of anti-Japanese sentiment on the island, illustrating the extent to which prejudice impacts the daily lives of the Japanese and Japanese American members of the community. As the previous chapters in the novel reveal, these prejudices are both subtle and overt, and the prosecution's characterization of Kabuo has repeatedly returned to the "sly and treacherous" stereotype of the Japanese and those of Japanese descent. And, this connection is, according to Kabuo, one that is pervasive among the white members of San Piedro Island.

Chapter 27 continues with Kabuo's revelation of what happened the night of Carl Jr.'s death. After Nels prompts his client to tell the truth, Kabuo admits, "the truth isn't easy" (392). The narrative then shifts to the past, a flashback to that night. Kabuo and Carl are both fishing in Ship Channel Bank. One of Carl's batteries is dead, and Carl sends out a distress signal. Kabuo answers the signal, and the two fishermen tie their boats together. Kabuo loans Carl one of his spare D-6 batteries, but the men realize that Carl's boat uses D-8 batteries. Carl uses Kabuo's fishing gaff as a hammer to bend the battery hold to accommodate Kabuo's spare battery. In the process, Carl cuts his hand, which explains the presence of his blood on the fishing gaff handle.

After the battery is installed, Carl thanks Kabuo, admitting that he might not have done the same for him. The conversation quickly centers on the sale of the seven acres, and Carl tells Kabuo that his mother sold the land while he was "fighting you goddamn Jap sons a ... " (404). Kabuo interrupts Carl, reminding him that he is "an American" and that Carl's German ancestry never caused Kabuo to refer to him as a "Nazi" (404). Carl apologizes and tells Kabuo that he still has the bamboo fishing rod Kabuo had given him before he was sent "off to prison camp" (405). Kabuo replies that Carl can keep the fishing rod. Carl then raises the issue of the land again, offering to sell Kabuo the land for the same price Zenhichi had negotiated with his father, Carl Sr. The two men agree on payment arrangements, and the chapter ends with Kabuo telling Carl, "it's a deal" (405).

Narratively speaking, the revelations of Chapter 27, which initially take place in a meeting between Nels and Kabuo in a prison cell, are subsequently transferred to the witness stand in **Chapter 28**, which opens with Kabuo finishing his testimony in court. Alvin Hooks cross-examines the defendant, and Kabuo admits that he did not initially tell the sheriff about his meeting with Carl Jr. the night of his death. The prosecutor presses Kabuo for more information about the battery. More specifically, Alvin Hooks asks Kabuo why, if he loaned Carl Jr. his spare battery, he had another spare battery in his boat the day it was searched by the sheriff and his deputy. Kabuo tells the prosecutor that he replaced the missing battery with one from his shed. When asked by Alvin Hooks why he didn't tell the sheriff about his meeting with the deceased the night before, Kabuo replies that he was unwilling to cooperate out of fear of being unfairly judged. Hooks reiterates, for the jury, the inconsistencies in Kabuo's testimony, stating, "you're a hard man to trust, Mr. Miyamoto ... You sit before us with no expression, keeping a poker face ... " (411–412). Hooks's statement is interrupted by Nels Gudmundsson, Judge Fielding tells the prosecutor that such statements are inappropriate. Alvin Hooks then concludes his interrogation of Kabuo.

The chapter ends with a significant observation by the omniscient narrator. According to the narrator:

Kabuo Miyamoto rose in the witness box so that the citizens in the gallery saw him fully—a Japanese man standing proudly before them, thick and strong through the torso.... While they watched he turned his dark eyes to the snowfall and gazed at it for a long time. The citizens in the gallery were reminded of photographs they had seen of Japanese soldiers ... He was, they decided, not like them at all, and the detached and aloof manner in which he watched the snowfall made this palpable and self-evident. (412)

This passage brings the reader back to the opening of the novel, for it resembles the initial description provided of the defendant. In spite of the testimony provided, the "citizens in the gallery" still view Kabuo as "Japanese" and not American. His physical appearance reminds them of "photographs.... of Japanese soldiers," and the citizens in the gallery decide that he is "not like them at all." Interestingly, the observation made by the omniscient narrator does not acknowledge the other "citizens" in attendance—the twenty-four Japanese and Japanese Americans who are initially mentioned in Chapter 7. Thus, the conclusion drawn by the narrator reflects the sentiments of the white citizens in the courtroom who still cling to the stereotypes of Japanese and Japanese Americans.

Chapter 29 begins with Alvin Hooks's closing remarks. According to the omniscient narrator, Hooks "characterized the accused man as a murderer in cold blood, one who had decided to kill another man and had executed his plan faithfully" (413). Hooks then urges the jury to consider the "facts" that have been presented about the night of Carl Jr.'s death. Hooks stresses the "treachery" of the defendant, a man who used "the code among fisherman to assist one another in times of trouble" (414) and his past friendship with Carl Jr. in order to board Carl Jr.'s boat and murder him. Hooks returns to this characterization of "treachery" repeatedly in his closing statements, and ends his speech to the jury with the following words of advice:

> We are talking about convicting a man of murder in the first degree. We are talking about *justice*, finally. We're talking about looking clearly at the defendant and seeing the truth self-evident in him and in the facts present in this case. Take a good look, ladies and gentleman, at the defendant sitting over there. Look into his eyes, consider his face, and ask yourselves what your duty is as citizens of this community. (415)

This passage marks the culmination of the prosecution's case and signals one of the major conflicts in *Snow Falling on Cedars*. Hooks, in asking the jury to consider the "self-evident" guilt of the defendant, recalls the closing moments of the previous chapter, when Kabuo left the witness stand and it was "self-evident" to the white citizens in the gallery that he is "not like them." Playing on this difference, Hooks reiterates Kabuo's otherness in this excerpt; he asks the members of the jury to look at Kabuo's physical attributes, which mark him as "Japanese." In looking at Kabuo's eyes and face, the jury is encouraged to consider this as evidence of his guilt and "treachery," and this argument historically resembles the one used to intern Japanese and Japanese Americans during World War II. Within the fictional space of the narrative, such connections have, as the previous chapters reveal, also greatly impacted the Japanese and Japanese American residents of San Piedro Island.

Nels Gudmundsson, in the same chapter, also provides his closing statements, and he attempts to counter the prosecution's assertion of "otherness" with a declaration of Kabuo's similarities to those who sit on the jury. More specifically, the defense attorney reminds the jury that:

> Kabuo Miyamoto *is* connected with [the war]. He is a much-decorated first lieutenant of the United States Army who fought for his country—the United States—in the European theater. If you see in his face a lack of emotion, if you see in him a silent pride, it is the pride and hollowness of a veteran of war who has returned home to *this*. He has returned to find himself the victim of prejudice—make no mistake about it, this trial is about prejudice—in the country he fought to defend. (417)

Thus, contrary to the prosecution's argument that Kabuo is representative of the enemy, Nels Gudmundsson stresses that his client is a citizen of the United States who fought valiantly for his country. Nels emphasizes that Kabuo is a citizen, a loyal citizen, of the United States, revealing to both the reader and the jury that the prosecution's case of "otherness" is based on stereotype and does not take into account the facts of Kabuo's character and past. As opposed to being the embodiment of "treachery," Nels points out that Kabuo is ultimately an

American representative of loyalty to his country. Nels then urges the jury to not let Kabuo's physical appearance influence their decision, and that they must "sentence him simply as an American, equal in the eyes of our legal system to every other American" (418).

Chapter 29 concludes with Judge Lewellen Fielding's reminder to the jury that Kabuo is charged with first-degree murder, and that a conviction requires a unanimous ruling. According to the judge, a guilty verdict should only be delivered if all the members of the jury are convinced of the defendant's guilt beyond a reasonable doubt. If there is any uncertainty, the jury is bound by law to find the defendant not guilty. Judge Fielding ends his statements to the jury with the assertion that "the storm ... is beyond our control, but the outcome of this trial is not ... " (422). This declaration is followed by the Judge's announcement that the trial is adjourned and instructs the jury to begin their deliberations, which marks the termination of the chapter.

As the jurors file out, **Chapter 30** begins in the courtroom, moments after the trial has been adjourned. Because of the storm, some of those observing the trial elect to linger in the courtroom, including Nels, Ishmael, and Hatsue. Ishmael reflects on Nels's closing statements, recognizing the legacy of the war and what he has lost in the ten years since the war. In an internal monologue, Ishmael compares the loss of his limb with the loss of Hatsue, and considers the role of history, which he concludes is "whimsical and immune to private yearnings" (425). Ishmael observes Hatsue in the courtroom, remembering the moments he had spent with her in the cedar tree. Ishmael's remembrance is broken by a comment from Nels Gudmundsson, who tells him that he greatly admired Ishamel's father, Arthur. Nels leaves, and Ishmael follows him out of the courtroom. Ishmael and Hisao, Hatsue's father, meet in the cloakroom, and Ishmael offers him a ride. Hisao thanks Ishmael and tells him that they have made other arrangements. Hatsue then enters the cloakroom and again asks Ishmael to publish a column about the trial in what she calls, "your father's newspaper" (426). Ishmael reminds Hatsue that it is his paper now, and tells her if she wants to speak about the issue further, that she can find him at his mother's house.

The narrative then shifts from the courtroom setting to the outdoors, as Ishmael makes his way to his car. The eye of the storm has passed, and, according to Ishmael, "the worst of it was behind them" (427). Thus, the conclusion of the storm coincides with the conclusion of the trial, which further emphasizes the connection between the storm and the trial. Ishmael relates the impact of the storm in his observations of the landscape, which is filled with uprooted trees, fallen branches, and capsized boats in the harbor. Ishmael then realizes that, "for the first time in his life ... such destruction could be beautiful" (428). Ishmael, with the maritime records in his pocket, is unsure how to proceed—he does not know, at this moment, whether to reveal the truth behind Carl's death or let the trial take its course.

Chapter 30 concludes with the deliberations of the jury. One of the jurors, Alexander Van Ness, doubts that Kabuo committed premeditated murder, thus holding up the verdict. The other jurors believe that Kabuo is indeed guilty of the crime, yet Alexander Van Ness, "a gray-bearded" boat builder who "lived out on Woodhouse Cove Road" in San Piedro Island (428), maintains that the evidence does not prove the defendant's guilt beyond a reasonable doubt. The other jurors present their reasons why they think Kabuo is guilty, and, in the process, they outline the case presented by prosecutor Alvin Hooks. However, the jurors are unsuccessful in swaying Alexander Van Ness. Frustrated, the jurors adjourn for the night, and the chapter ends without a decision of a unanimous guilty verdict.

Chapter 31 returns the narrative's focus to Ishmael, who has gone to his mother's house. Ishmael goes into his father's study, surrounded by books, and considers his father's character and reputation. He remembers his father's assertion that, "An enemy on an island is an enemy forever" (439), and reflects on his father's seemingly contradictory love and dislike of the San Piedro community. This particular statement has powerful implications in *Snow Falling on Cedars*, for it echoes the revelations made in preceding chapters. More specifically, as Kabuo's trial illustrates, the perception of "an enemy," and, in this instance, of the "Japanese enemy," still persists despite the passage of time. And, this conflict is difficult to mediate, because the isolation of the island, and the interdependence such an isolation creates among its residence, makes it a place where sentiments can easily become magnified and contradictory viewpoints often remain suppressed for the relative good of the community. According to Arthur Chambers, the islanders often "held their breath and walked with care" (439). Thus, the islanders, in Arthur Chambers's assessment, often hide in silence because such a position doesn't easily allow the community as a whole to question its motivations and actions. In spite of its flaws, Arthur Chambers had a contradictory relationship with the San Piedro community, for he both loved the island and often disliked the actions of its inhabitants.

Ishmael comes to a similar conclusion about the San Piedro community in Chapter 31, realizing that what initially appears to be a black and white issue is often a more complicated shade of gray. In recognizing the ambiguity of life on the island and its inhabitants, Ishmael acknowledges that he is "his father's son." This intergenerational connection is physically manifest in the fact that Ishmael sits "in the same spindle-based Windsor chair ... his father had brooded in" (439). It is in this moment of reflection that Ishmael recalls an interaction he and his father had with Mr. Fukida, a Japanese resident of San Piedro, at the annual Strawberry Festival. Mr. Fukida and Arthur discuss their families, and Arthur tells Mr. Fukida that he has "high hopes" for Ishmael. Mr. Fukido agrees with Arthur's assertion, replying that he "believe[s] his heart is strong, like his father's" (441). This remembrance is immediately interrupted by the present-time actions of Ishmael, who leaves the study and goes into his room. Ishmael rereads Hatsue's letter, coming to a far different conclusion than the one reached in Chapter 24. More specifically, Ishmael focuses his attention on the closing moments of the letter, in which Hatsue writes:

I wish you the very best, Ishmael. Your heart is large and you are gentle and kind, and I know you will do great things in this world, but now I must say good-bye to you. I am going to move on with my life the best I can, and I hope you will too. (442)

Ishmael realizes that Hatsue had once admired him for his heart, and that, since the war, her expectation of him has been left unfulfilled. His bitterness and his inability to move on are at the root of the tension in their relationship, and Ishmael recognizes that it is he, not Hatsue, who must change. Ishmael, after reading the letter, ventures outside the house, and he walks to the cedar tree, recognizing that he "had no place in the tree any longer" (443). This marks a significant moment in the protagonist's journey to reconciling the past, for Ishmael finally realizes that his youth, and the relationship he shared with Hatsue, is something that has ended and that he can no longer live in the past. Ishmael eventually walks toward the Imada house, armed with the intention to reveal the truth to Hatsue and her family about the night of Carl Jr.'s death. Chapter 31 ends with this revelation.

The final chapter of the novel takes place in the Imada house, after Ishmael has told Hatsue and her family about the maritime report. Hatsue, grateful for Ishmael's help, kisses him on the cheek. She tells him, "Find someone to marry ... Have children, Ishmael. Live." This action marks the ultimate reconciliation between Ishmael and Hatsue. Ishmael's decision to reveal the truth also signals his growth as a character. Ishmael is finally able to actively engage with the present, and this is the first time in the narrative that he has affected change as opposed to passively contemplating the past. His decision to help Hatsue and Kabuo also represents his acceptance of the past, and his action is heroic in scope. It is he, after all, who is responsible for saving Kabuo's life, and it is his willingness to take a stand that will finally change the course of the trial. On another level, Ishmael's statement contradicts the dominant communal notion of Kabuo's guilt, and his stand resembles the one taken by his father during the internment. Thus, Ishmael is able to enact, on the individual level, a reconciliation of past wrongs committed against the Japanese and Japanese American community. Moreover, Ishmael, in performing this act, becomes an admirable, honorable figure like his father.

Chapter 32 continues into the following morning. Hatsue visits Ishmael, who tells him that Kabuo had, in his testimony, alluded to the fact that Carl had tied a lantern to his mast because he had no electricity to power the lights on his boat. Hatsue deduces that, if the lantern is still tied to the mast, Kabuo will be absolved of the murder charge—if the lantern is found, Kabuo's story about the dead battery will have physical evidence. Hatsue and Ishmael then leave for the sheriff's office, and, with the maritime report in hand, tell Art Moran about their findings. Art agrees to revisit the crime scene, and the three, along with the deputy, Abel Martinson, go to Carl's boat, which has been kept in sealed storage. Art doesn't allow Hatsue into the storage area. Ishmael, Art and Abel investigate the boat. Though no lantern is found, there is some twine on the mast, which indicates that something was tied to it. There is also some blood on the mast. Ishmael suggests to Art that this finding is further evidence of Kabuo's innocence. Ishmael reasons that, after Kabuo had left, Carl might have cut the lantern from the mast. The blood found reflects the fact that Carl had cut his hand installing the battery. Ishmael speculates that the wake of the freighter may have knocked Carl off the mast while he was cutting the lantern loose, which would explain the absence of the lantern. The men, after closely inspecting the boat, do find a "small fracture in the wood" in the "port side gunnel just below the mast" (454). It is in this small fracture that they find three small hairs, which prove, without a doubt, that Carl's death is an accident and not a murder. The hairs are taken to Horace Whaley, who confirms that they do indeed belong to the deceased. The evidence is then presented to Judge Lewellen Fielding, who dismisses the charges against Kabuo.

As *Snow Falling on Cedars* draws to a close, the reader is left with Ishmael's narrative about the night of Carl Jr.'s death, which will appear in the *San Piedro Review*. According to

Ishmael's account, which represents the final flashback moment in the novel, Carl Jr. spent his last moments at sea, alone. As the freighter moved into Ship Bank Channel, Carl Jr. climbed up the mast to remove the lantern. In the space of minutes, he was thrown overboard by the freighter's wake, and he subsequently hit his head and drowned. Simultaneously, Kabuo, in another part of the ocean, spent his night fishing, and eventually returned home to tell his wife about the land he had finally reclaimed. And, soon after, Kabuo was arrested and charged for a crime he did not commit. The narrative then shifts from the past to a present-day recollection, as Ishmael pauses with "fingertips poised just above the keys" (460). Ishmael's final account is perhaps the most significant part of the novel, for it encapsulates the thematic foci of the novel. According to the omniscient narrator, Ishmael understood that "accident ruled every corner of the universe except the chambers of the human heart" (460). Thus, though the force of history and the power of nature may overwhelm communities like San Piedro Island, there is a power and an agency in the individual, who can still perform acts of compassion and forgiveness.

Notes

1. The 1790 naturalization law dictated that only "free white persons" could obtain citizenship. After 1870, the law was amended to include "those of African descent," but was not applicable to Asian immigrants. This law was eventually amended in 1952, by the McCarren-Walter Act, and it wasn't until the passage of this act that Asian immigrants could apply and receive naturalized citizenship in the United States.

2. Japanese American troops were among the most decorated during World War II. For example, members of the 442nd and 100th received distinction for their efforts on European front, and served in spite of the prejudice that existed in their home country.

3. "Nisei" is a term used for second generation Japanese Americans.

Works Cited

Guterson, David. *Snow Falling on Cedars*. New York: Vintage Books, 1995.

Critical Views

MICHAEL HARRIS ON MULTIPLE LAYERS
AND ETHICS

David Guterson's haunting first novel works on at least two levels. It gives us a puzzle to solve—a whodunit complete with courtroom maneuvering and surprising turns of evidence—and at the same time it offers us a mystery, something altogether richer and deeper.

In 1954, off the island of San Piedro in Puget Sound, salmon fisherman Carl Heine is found drowned and entangled in his boat's gill net. It seems to be an accident. Soon, however, darker suspicions bubble to the surface, and a fisherman of Japanese descent, Kabuo Miyomoto, is put on trial for murder.

Heine, the coroner discovers, has a fractured skull; before drowning, he hit his head on something, or was hit. Evidence confirms that Miyomoto boarded Heine's boat on the foggy night when he died-a rare occurrence among these solitary and self-reliant men. Yet Miyomoto's initial statements to investigators failed to mention such a visit. Besides, Miyomoto had a motive for foul play. When San Piedro's Japanese population was interned in 1942, his parents had nearly paid off their mortgage on a seven-acre strawberry farm bought from Heine's parents. Heine's mother, Etta, promptly sold the land to another farmer. Stoic in the face of legalized injustice, Miyomoto and his wife, Hatsue, waited patiently to repurchase the farm when its owner grew old, but instead Heine bought it just before his death.

This is the puzzle: We are led to believe that Miyomoto, who fought with the legendary 442nd Regimental Combat Team in Europe, is an honorable man, although his stern bearing revives anti-Japanese prejudices that nine postwar years have only lightly buried. We are led to believe that distrust of whites—his family and Hatsue's were shipped to the Manzanar camp in California's Owens Valley—and guilt over the German soldiers he has killed make him accept his arrest as fate.

But if Miyomoto is innocent, why does a net of circumstantial evidence bind him as tightly as any struggling fish?

Ishmael Chambers covers the trial for San Piedro's newspaper, which he inherited from his father. A former Marine who lost an arm fighting the Japanese at Tarawa, Chambers was Hatsue's high school sweetheart; before her crowning as Strawberry Festival Princess in 1941, they secretly met and necked in a hollow cedar tree. From Manzanar, however, Hatsue wrote denying that she loved him, and in the Pacific he felt his love turn into hate. By now, love and hate alike have faded. "You went numb, Ishmael," his mother tells him. "And you've stayed numb all these years."

Just as Miyomoto is obsessed with getting back the exact acreage that his family lost, so Chambers sleepwalks through life in the vague hope of reclaiming Hatsue. The contrast between these two obsessions—one conscious and potentially fruitful, the other unconscious and debilitating—is Guterson's main device for leading us into the mystery. Which is: How can people in a small, tightly knit community be neighbors for generations, even love one another, yet be torn apart by racism?

During the three-day trial, an epochal snowstorm intensifies San Piedro's isolation. Island people, Chambers' father once told him, can't afford to make enemies.

"No one trod easily upon the emotions of another.... This was excellent and poor at the same time-excellent because most people took care, poor because it meant an inbreeding of the spirit, too much held in, regret and silent brooding ... fear of opening up." The ordeal of the storm, coupled with the shock of Heine's death, forces them to confront the past and cracks the ice of their reserve.

Guterson (whose previous work includes a story collection, "The Country Ahead of Us, the Country Behind") convinces us that he knows or has researched everything essential here-details of fishing, farming and lawyering; of Coast Guard and coroner's procedures; of Japanese American culture.

With a stately pace and an old-fashioned omniscient voice, he describes the beauty of the Puget Sound islands, the bloody chaos of Tarawa, the desolation of Manzanar and the inner life of every major character.

What he finds there is usually nobility. The only semi-villains are Etta Heine, a couple of FBI men and the anonymous callers who curse Chambers' father for his editorials defending the island's Japanese residents after Pearl Harbor.

Everyone else—Hatsue, Heine's widow, the judge, the sheriff, the aged defense attorney, tough and silent Heine himself—is human and often admirable.

How can so many good people coexist with a major historical evil? The mystery remains even after the puzzle is satisfyingly solved.

PICO IYER ON THE CLASHING OF CULTURES

"An enemy on an island is an enemy forever," muses one character in David Guterson's luminous first novel. That is another way of saying there are no hiding places on a relatively small island: everyone is forced to be conscious of others and the need to be removed from others. In the San Juan Islands of Puget Sound in the early 1950s, both the residents of Japanese descent and the"American" communities are further divided and shadowed by their recent memories of war.

(...)

Guterson's particular gift is for description: he takes you into one fully researched scene after another—gill-netters at work, an autopsy, digging for geoduck clams. With equal precision, Guterson traces the shadow lives of Japanese in the Northwest at a time when Americans of Japanese descent were referred to by Census takers as "Jap Number 1 ... laughing Jap, dwarf Jap ..." Set among the amputees and other casualties of war, in fact, the novel becomes a tender examination of fairness and forgiveness. The "Americans" come to seem as inscrutable as the Japanese, as clannish and as sparing with their feelings. And the divisions between the two are only intensified by their affinities: when the reticent descendants of samurai meet laconic Scandinavian fishermen, one form of silence glances off another. Toward the end, Guterson describes a lighthouse room that "smelled of salt water and snow and of the past," and that is very much the aroma of his richly atmospheric novel. Though movie ready in its pacing and narrative vividness, it is also unusually lived in, focused and compassionate. As its title suggests, *Snow Falling on Cedars* is poised at precisely that point where an elliptical Japanese delicacy meets the woody, unmoving fiber of the Pacific Northwest. Out of that encounter, Guterson has fashioned something haunting and true.

SUSAN KENNEY ON THE ROLE OF MEMORY

In March 1942, just before the 800 Japanese residents of San Piedro Island in Puget Sound are herded off to a California internment camp, 18-year-old Hatsue Imada gives what seems a naive response to her mother's description of the deep racial bias that has surfaced in their small, isolated community in the wake of Pearl Harbor: "They don't all hate us," Hatsue says. "You're exaggerating, mother, you know you are. They're not so different from us, you know. Some hate, others don't. It isn't all of them." Hatsue should know; for four years she has been carrying on a clandestine romance with a boy named Ishmael Chambers, son of the local newspaper editor, the two of them meeting at odd moments in a huge old hollow cedar in the forest between their houses. But neither the romance nor the friendship that they have shared since childhood will survive the bitter division brought about by the war.

Successive waves of wayward souls and eccentrics— Canadian Englishmen, Scots-Irish, Scandinavians, Germans and most recently Japanese, who came originally as migrant labor to pick berries on the extensive strawberry fields and stayed on, aspiring for their American-born children to own their own plots have resulted in an ethnically if not economically diverse population on this island of five thousand damp souls. Their isolation within the spectacularly beautiful but harsh environment has fostered the illusion of community, an illusion abruptly shattered by the advent of World War II.

It's now the first week in December 1954, and snow is falling outside the courtroom in the rainy, wind-beaten sea village of Amity Harbor, the island's only town, downtrodden and mildewed, where Hatsue's husband, Kabuo Miyomoto, is on trial. He is charged with the first-degree murder of Carl Heine, a fellow fisherman, whose body was found early on the morning of Sept. 16, entangled in his own gill net. Now the sole proprietor of his late father's newspaper, Ishmael Chambers, maimed both physically and psychically fighting against the Japanese in the South Pacific, looks out at the storm, hoping it will snow recklessly and bring to the island the impossible winter purity, so rare and precious, he remembered fondly from his youth.

But the war has taken a terrible toll on the human spirit, and memories of that desperate conflict have exacerbated the racial intolerance subtly present even before the war. This is most clearly evidenced in the testimony of Carl's mother. Etta Heine, whose act in denying the Miyomoto family ownership of their all-but-paid-for seven acres of strawberry fields is revealed as the first link in a decade-long chain of events that has now apparently culminated in Carl's death at the hands of Kabuo.

Though the courtroom setting defines the present in *Snow Falling on Cedars*, David Guterson's finely wrought and flawlessly written first novel (he is the author of a book of short stories and a guide to home schooling), this meticulously drawn legal drama forms only the topmost layer of complex time strata, which Mr. Guterson proceeds to mine assiduously through an intricate series of flashbacks. Thus testimony slides ineluctably from merely verbal recollection into remembered incident into fully realized historical narrative past events told from the numerous characters' points of view with all the detail and intensity of lives being lived before our very eyes.

The most immediate of these serial flashbacks recounts not only Sheriff Art Moran's investigation of the events surrounding Carl's death during the months preceding the trial, but also the personal histories of the people Moran has seen fit to interview and who are now being called as witnesses. Even minor characters Ole Jurgensen, present owner of the disputed seven acres; Horace Whaley, the coroner; Carl's wife, Susan Marie; Army Sgt. Victor Maples, who testifies to Kabuo's expertise in kendo, the ancient military art of the samurai warrior are dramatized well beyond their roles as participants in the trial.

Unlike many recent purveyors of courtroom calisthenics, Mr. Guterson does not stop there. Taking us back nearly a dozen years in both historical and personal time, he depicts the Allied invasion of the South Pacific island of Betio through the eyes of the 19-year-old Ishmael, as, lying gravely wounded on the beach, he sees the rest of his company wiped out, so that like his namesake he alone survives to tell the tale. Almost simultaneously, we accompany Hatsue and her family on their harrowing journey southward to California, and we share their deprivation and humiliation in the notorious internment camp of Manzanar, as well as the irony of Kabuo's turnabout military service fighting Germans in the European theater. Tunneling back even further, we witness Ishamel and Hatsue's secret meetings inside the hollow cedar, the development of their forbidden romance and its subsequent demise, adding emotional depth to their estrangement in the present.

As the exhaustive list of acknowledgments demonstrates, Mr. Guterson has done his homework on everything from autopsies to Zen Buddhism, taking on the enormous risk of crossing boundaries not just of time, but of sex and culture as well. The result is a densely packed, multifaceted work that sometimes hovers on the verge of digressiveness, but in Mr. Guterson's skilled hands never succumbs to the fragmentation that might well have marred such an ambitious undertaking. In fact, so compelling is the narrative that we almost lose sight of the central issue, which is, as the defense attorney Nels Gudmundsson reminds us in his summation, whether Kabuo Miyomoto is on trial for murder even worse, will be found guilty simply because he is Japanese.

Simply is not the right word. In a parallel to the case against Kabuo, the reader must sift back through the weight of the whole novel to determine not only whether Kabuo's accusation and trial are in fact racially motivated, but where the responsibility lies if this is in fact the case. Along with the clear manifestations of racism, there is enough evidence of people struggling with their own consciences, speaking out against prejudice, among them Ishmael's parents and Carl Heine's father, to support Hatsue's perception that it isn't all of them that hate.

The answer, finally, is equivocal at best. Is Kabuo's refusal to reveal his whereabouts on the fateful night a response to the prejudice he feels will condemn him out of hand, or a self-fulfilling prophecy that is in itself a form of racism? The key, Mr. Guterson seems to say, lies in the possibility of individual action. As Nels Gudmundsson instructs the jury: Your task as you deliberate together on these proceedings is to insure that you do nothing to yield to a universe in which things go awry by happenstance. Let fate, coincidence and accident conspire; human beings must act on reason.

In a heart-stopping demonstration of this, fate, coincidence and accident do conspire to supply a crucial bit of last-minute evidence, requiring one of the actors in this drama to choose whether to act on reason and compassion, or, by giving in to hatred and anger, let accident rule every corner of the universe. Thus the mystery plays itself out, along with the storm, leaving the human heart to shake free, as the hardiest cedars shake free of snow, of the chill of hatred and war if it only will.

CAROL HERMAN ON THE COURTROOM STRUCTURE

Imagine Earl Stanley Gardner collaborating with D.H. Lawrence to produce a novel with extravagantly suggestive, poetic language.

Imagine Rupert Birkin from "Women in Love" in the courtroom. Or better yet, imagine Perry Mason in Puget Sound.

In "Snow Falling on Cedars," David Guterson takes what appears to be formulaic crime and trial fiction and turns it on its head. There is some good lawyering, some breathtaking natural imagery and love and sex and ideas. For these violent, court-centered times, the novel is a canny, literate, passionate alternative to the current media extravaganzas where justice, as a concept, seems to vanish.

Set in an island town in the Pacific Northwest, the book opens with the trial of Kabuo Miyamoto, a Japanese-American fisherman accused of killing another fisherman, Carl Heine. Heine has been found drowned in his own net with a mysterious wound to his head. It is 1954 and Kabuo appears to have a motive.

Shortly before the start of World War II, Kabuo's family purchased seven acres of land from the Heine family, making all but the final payment. Then the Japanese bombed Pearl Harbor, and Kabuo's family was interned. It was Kabuo's desire to regain what he believed to be rightfully his, a desire that some members of the Heine family met with resistance.

In addition to the land dispute, there are several pieces of circumstantial evidence working against Kabuo. The most damning appears to be the nature of the blow to Carl's head. The coroner, who survived Okinawa, was reported to have said to the county sheriff that "if he were inclined to play Sherlock Holmes he ought to start looking for a Jap with a bloody gun butt—a right-handed Jap to be precise."

With the courtroom drama as his centerpiece, Mr. Guterson slowly and methodically reveals layers of information about Carl Heine's death and about relations between the white and Japanese communities on San Piedro island—the most passionate of which is the thwarted prewar love affair between Hatsue Miyamoto, Kabuo's wife, and Ishmael Chambers, the publisher and editor of the town newspaper.

Ishmael is a veteran who lost his arm in the war. With the trial, Ishmael is brought close once again to Hatsue. He recalls their earlier love affair, an affair that evolved slowly from picking strawberries to languid embraces in the hollow of an old cedar tree. It is his detective work that propels the intricate plot to its satisfying conclusion

(...)

The accumulating, and then the melting of snow becomes a metaphor for getting to the truth of Kabuo's guilt or innocence and for uncovering the larger question of one community's sense of justice. There are a number of ways to interpret the title, but the best way, I think, is suggested by Hatsue in a flashback to when her father was arrested after Pearl Harbor:

> "To deny that there was this dark side of life would be like pretending that the cold of winter was somehow only a temporary illusion, a way station on the way to the higher 'reality' of long, warm, pleasant summers. But summer it turned out was no more real than the snow that melted in wintertime."

The dark side of this novel is undeniable. So is its grace. For all the poetry and courtroom razzle—dazzle that one finds here, Mr. Guterson has let the facts about the internment of Japanese—Americans speak for themselves. In the end, he retrieves an important, if bleak, part of this country's history, and he does it not as a lawyer or a visionary, but as a reporter:

> "The Kobayashis—they'd planted a thousand dollars' worth of rhubarb on five acres in Center Valley—negotiated an agreement with Torval Rasmussen to tend and harvest their crop. The Masuis weeded their strawberry fields and worked at staking peas in the moonlight; they wanted to leave things in good condition for Michael Burns and his ne'er-do-well brother Patrick, who'd agreed to take care of their farm. The Sumidas decided to sell at cut-rate and close their nursery down."

Beyond the courtroom of this novel, there is a universe of human aspiration and despair. There is love and disappointment and history and endurance. Justice is redeemed.

NANCY PATE ON COMMUNITY AND JUSTICE

It is December of 1954, and in the crowded courthouse on the Puget Sound island of San Piedro, a man is on trial for murder. Outside, a winter storm is brewing, the wind from the sea driving the snowflakes inland. Soon, the snow quietly blankets the island-much like the silent prejudice that shrouds its "five thousand damp souls."

The man accused of murdering salmon fisherman Carl Heine is another fisherman, Kabuo Miyomoto. He and Carl went to school together, but then Kabuo, like the 843 people of Japanese descent who lived on San Piedro in March of 1942, was exiled to the Manzanar internment camp. There he married a fellow islander, Hatsue, before joining the U.S. Army and fighting in Europe. After the war, Kabuo and Hatsue returned to San Piedro with dreams of having their own strawberry farm, only to find that Carl's mother, Etta, had foreclosed on the seven acres that Kabuo's late father had been buying. This loss of the land, and a more recently foiled attempt to buy it again, is supposedly the motive for Kabuo having boarded Carl's fishing boat in the fog, bashed him on the head and pitched him overboard.

Listening to the state present its case, local reporter Ishmael Chambers, who lost an arm in the war, remembers the past. He went to school with Carl and Kabuo. But it was Hatsue who was his childhood friend, his teenage love, the girl he planned to marry in the innocent days before Pearl Harbor.

David Guterson's carefully crafted first novel provides more than just courtroom drama. As the trial proceeds, he essentially puts the island on trial, alternating chapters of testimony and cross-examination with flashbacks—to the idyllic days when Ishmael and Hatsue dug for clams and wandered in the woods, to the deprivations of desolate Manzanar, to the horrors of war, to the investigation into Carl Heine's death. Prejudice takes many forms: the outright venom of Etta Heine; white fishermen joking that they can't tell one Japanese-American from another; islanders passively watching as their neighbors are loaded on ferries in Amity Harbor.

Guterson's prose is controlled and graceful, almost detached. But the accretion of small details gives his story weight. He's particularly good at evoking a sense of place—the yellow dust cloaking the barbed wire and barracks of Manzanar, the strawberry-scented summer on San Piedro, the slippery, kerosene-lanterned deck of a fishing boat at night. Then there is the snow falling on cedars. As the snow buries the island, Guterson's narrative begins to reveal the community's secret heart, the injustice that may break it in two.

LUCY HUGHES-HALLETT ON THE ROLE OF RACE AND RACISM

It is 1954. A Japanese-American, who has spent his war years fighting in Europe, is accused of the murder of a German-American who fought in the Pacific against the "Japs". David Guterson's first novel, a skillfully constructed, deeply affecting story of love and death, is set on a small island (population "five thousand damp souls") off-shore from Seattle. It's an inward-looking place where nothing much ever happens, but the novel's real subject is an international one, the unquantifiable but dire after-effects of war.

Carl Heine and Kabuo Miyamoto played together as boys. Their fathers were both strawberry farmers. Kabuo's father rented, and hoped eventually to buy, land from Carl's. As adults they are fishermen, members of a fleet of slow-spoken salmon-netters who work alone but whose lives may depend on each other's help at sea. Both of them have been damaged by their wartime experiences, not as obviously as Ishmael, the local newspaperman who lost an arm, but none the less fundamentally. They are both in their different ways taciturn, edgy. Neither has friends. When Heine is found drowned, tangled in his own net with an odd-shaped dent in his skull, suspicion falls on Miyamoto.

There is a motive. Old Mrs Heine sold off the land the Miyamotos considered theirs, profiting ruthlessly by their internment. There is also the fact of Kabuo's ethnic identity.

"You look like one of Tojo's soldiers," his wife tells him during a court recess. "You'd better quit sitting up so straight and tall." He is strong, dignified, impassive. He looks like the enemy.

The narrative follows the trial, but this is not a courtroom drama. The question of whether Kabuo did or did not kill Carl Heine is far less pressing than that of whether his neighbours will be fair to him, and of whether Ishmael, the hero, Kabuo's rival in love, will deal honourably with the piece of essential evidence he has happened across. Guterson uses the witnesses and their testimony as pegs securing an ably contrived web of flashbacks. The emotional centre of the book is in the subplot, the love story of Ishmael and the beautiful Japanese girl Hatsue, who eventually rejects him to marry one of her own kind.

Guterson's world is richly imagined, full of practical and sensuous detail. He is good on manual work, on the smells of fish and strawberries and cedar, on the gruesome details of an autopsy. The community he conjures up is various and vital. His bit-part players are as engaging and clearly delineated as his principles. The aging dandy of a defence counsel, Ishmael's sturdy God-fearing mother, the fussy, nervous sheriff with his passion for Juicy Fruit gum: each one is vividly and economically realised.

They are all, with the exception of Carl Heine's mother, essentially decent. This is a warm-hearted, heart-warming book. The officers of the law may not be brilliant, but they are men of probity. We never really doubt that Ishmael, embittered though we have been told he is, will do the right thing. We never really suspect Kabuo, angry as we know him to be.

But Guterson is not a sentimental optimist. His account of the assault on a Japanese-occupied Pacific island, in which Ishmael loses his arm, is clear-eyed and terrible. His rendering of small-island life is enriched by his awareness of meanness and jealousy as well as by his respect for his characters' strengths. This is a hugely attractive book, written in clipped, elegant prose, and all the more enjoyable for its measure of sadness and regret.

JANE MENDELSOHN ON HATSUE'S CHARACTER

The novel comes closest to transcending its good intentions in the story of Ishmael and Hatsue. Ishmael is the novel's conscience; he's the one with the secrets and the moral dilemma. He's Henry Fonda. As a boy, he and Hatsue dug clams together, grew up, and eventually became secret sweethearts, hidden from their families and friends. But when Pearl Harbour happens, their love is tested: Hatsue finds it wanting while Ishmael finds it deeper than ever and proposes. Sent to the camps, Hatsue writes to him, breaking off their relationship and admitting that she doesn't love him. Ishmael goes off to war, loses an arm, and when he returns, he is a bitter loner and she is married.

Guterson weaves Ishmael and Hatsue's memories seamlessly into the fabric of the trial and he lets their story breathe with real passion. He describes their trysts in the hollow of a cedar tree and their final parting at the edge of a strawberry field with aching, unsentimental emotion. And he creates in Hatsue Miyamoto a truly complex character. Beautiful, intelligent, caught between her Japanese heritage and American upbringing, Hatsue struggles internally more than any other character with the tensions between the two cultures. Guterson really understands Hatsue, and, finally, we realise, he puts her at the centre of the storm in this book; she is its real heroine.

Hatsue gives *Snow Falling On Cedars* a life-affirming, unneurotic quality which is absent from so much fiction, and which makes such a traditional novel seem almost dull. (Compare Guterson's Ishmael with his more colourful ancestor.) Yet when Hatsue whispers to Ishmael toward the end of the book, "Have children, Ishmael. Live.", the simple message doesn't sound dull at all, but inspiring and wise.

SUZANNE MANTELL ON THE PUBLISHING HISTORY

Topping the November 27 and December 11 PW trade paperback bestseller list, above *Calvin & Hobbes* and *Chicken*

Soup for the Soul, there stood *Snow Falling on Cedars*, David Guterson's finely wrought first novel about a Japanese American fisherman formerly interned during World War II on trial for murder. Vintage, which brought out the paper edition in October, reports 12 printings in five weeks, with more than 460,000 copies in print its fastest-selling novel ever.

When literary novels top the charts, it usually requires a confluence of circumstances especially word of mouth. You feel uplifted when you finish reading it, says Anne Borchardt, Guterson's agent, citing the appeal of *Snow Falling on Cedars* gripping plot, strong characters and a sense of moral order. Even the author, returning from a book tour in England, where *Snow* has sold 180,000 copies, concluded that word of mouth was his prime ally. The book has sold to publishers in 10 other countries.

But a look at the book's history indicates that word of mouth was just one element on the road to bestsellerdom. Several other factors, some planned, some not, combined to make the book a hit.

Vintage claims much of the credit, saying it got behind thebook early. Barnes & Noble also claims a role, having singled out *Snow* for special recognition. Harcourt and Vintage praise the independents for their embrace of the novel. The author notes that he's worked hard for the book's awards and reception. Knowing novelist Charles Johnson (*Middle Passage*) hasn't hurt either.

The saga started in early 1994, when Harcourt Brace announced that it was significantly scaling back its adult trade division. "They already had the rights to my book," Guterson explains by phone from his home on Bainbridge Island in Puget Sound, Washington, a place not unlike *Snow*'s fictional setting. "I was getting nervous that their commitment wouldn't be there. A lot of people left. But when Harcourt shifted its focus again," Guterson recalls, "they made a commitment to my book. My editor [Alane Mason, now at Norton] was still there. The sales reps got excited. I got optimistic. Then Mason left, and I got nervous again. But things were already in place and the book was treated very well."

Snow got excellent prepub reviews, and Harcourt planned a 25,000 first printing and a major author tour. Upon publication in October, the book again got good reviews, and HB increased its marketing commitment. "It was good timing," Guterson adds. "It's a good Christmas book because of the title and the cover picture. Sales were good. Then it got quiet."

In the spring, though, *Snow* revived. It won the Barnes & Noble Discovery Award, then the PEN/Faulkner Award for Fiction. It also was nominated for the 1943 adult trade ABBY Award by the American Booksellers Association and won the Pacific Northwest Booksellers Award.

The book racked up substantial sales in Seattle, San Francisco and other western cities, helped along by glowing reviews plus a blurb from Johnson, Guterson's former teacher at the University of Washington and, as it happens, one of the three judges for the PEN Award.

When B&N chose *Snow* for its second annual Discover Award, it positioned it in the fiction section and promoted it up front. Joining the buyers in the choice were authors Frank Conroy, Russell Banks and James Wilcox.

Barnes & Noble, very much more than anyone, put *Snow Falling on Cedars* on the map, asserts B & N chief operating officer Steve Riggio. We sold a disproportionate number of copies [30,000] for the total number of sales, which have neared 70,000 copies.

Snow's success in the West was duplicated elsewhere, especially Washington, D.C., after the Washington Post's David Streitfeld highlighted the book and the paper excerpted Guterson's PEN/Faulkner acceptance speech. While the Faulkner award is a solid endorsement from the literary community, it doesn't always guarantee a sales surge; however, the PEN/Faulkner Foundation, at Vintage's request, had designed an attention-getting prize sticker for use on the paper edition. As Guterson says, "Basically it was a long ride from last fall to this summer, with good sales and some surges. Then Vintage took over."

Before Mason left Harcourt, she had lunch with Vintage editor Robin Desser (now at Knopf), and handed Desser galleys for Snow. Desser recalls: "The book had authority, lyricism, an incredible narrative. It didn't miss a beat. And it had a political context. I fell head over heels for it." She gave the galleys to Vintage chief Marty Asher, who agreed to put down a modest floor for paperback rights. The brilliant thing would have been to have paid a lot for the rights right then, before the book took off, Desser says. I paid a lot more at auction, but I don't think I overpaid. The sale was for six figures, with an option on Guterson's next novel, tentatively titled *East of the Mountains*, which Harcourt's Drenka Willen recently bought on the basis of an outline and a chapter while Guterson was being wooed by the other houses.

Desser took the unusual step of distributing hardcover copies to the Vintage sales force even before she had bought the book; later, the house sent 6000 copies of its 86,000 first printing to key accounts.

(...)

Guterson says Manhattan publishing types call the book's saga refreshing. People in New York are so cynical, they like the idea of a complete unknown working in Puget Sound whose book makes it on the basis of its own merit, he says. But the 39-year-old author sees his writing career as a gradual, steady progression, from complete anonymity to where I am now.

JUDITH BROMBERG ON GUTERSON'S USE OF MEMORY

The courtroom proceedings are the pegs upon which Guterson hangs the memories, grudges, disappointments, omissions, commissions, and, yes, the kindnesses, cordialities and generosities of the longtime inhabitants of this closed island community—two communities, actually. A small cadre of Japanese-American strawberry farmers lived separate but parallel lives to the mainstream population of the island; parallel, that is, until Pearl Harbor and the internment; afterward, just separate.

One of the two main story lines undergirding the trial concerns the attempt by the father of Kabuo Miyamoto several years before the war to purchase from Carl Heine Sr., the father of the deceased, seven acres of the strawberry plot he farmed. Zenhichi Miyamoto was one payment away from owning the land outright when "security concerns" warranted the removal of all Americans of Japanese descent into the internment camps. Shortly thereafter, Carl Sr. died, his widow returned to the Miyamotos the money already paid and resold her entire acreage to a third party.

Since returning to San Piedro after the war, it had been a tenacious dream of Kabuo to repurchase the plot that he believed was morally and ethically—if not legally—his. Carl Jr. and Kabuo had grown up side by side. In fact, up to his death, Carl had kept a memento Kabuo had given him just before leaving for Manzanar. Since the war, however, they had had little to do with each other, except that Kabuo, understanding that Carl was about to regain possession of his family farm, visited Carl at his home the day before Carl died to try to renegotiate with him the purchase, once again, of those seven acres.

The other story line centers on the friendship that grew up into a love affair between Hatsue Imada, now Kabuo's wife, and Ishmael Chambers, then son of the newspaper owner/editor, now owner/editor himself. They would meet furtively in the hollow of a huge cedar until the Imada family was also relocated to Manzanar. Ishmael recarved that cedar in his heart, causing him both pleasure and pain. Later, the war he fought in the Pacific claimed another part of him, and even though peace broke out, it never happened to Ishmael.

Arthur Chambers at one point observed that, in an island community, "no one trod easily on the emotions of another where the sea licked everywhere against an endless shoreline. And this was excellent and poor at the same time—excellent because it meant most people took care, poor because it meant an inbreeding of the spirit, too much held in, regret and silent brooding, a world where inhabitants walked in fear and trepidation, in fear of opening up."

The storm subsided as the trial was nearing its conclusion. Ishmael Chambers walked the island breathing in the destruction, awestruck by the terrible beauty of the place. "It occurred to Ishmael for the first time in his life that such destruction could be beautiful." And with this realization Ishmael grasped the truth of his father's reflection on how the island shaped the course of many lives.

Guterson's handling of metaphor and motif—the cedars, snow and storm, strawberries, the sea and salmon—enriches both plot and theme. His characters are fully drawn, fully human and his manipulation of setting, specifically the island of San Piedro, elevates it to that of another significant player in this drama.

JAMES H. MEREDITH ON HISTORY AND THE FICTIONAL HOME FRONT

Winner of the 1996 American Booksellers Book of the Year award, this novel is about the dramatic changes that occurred in Amity Harbor, a small community on San Piedro Island in the Pacific Northwest, when America entered the war. After the Japanese surprise attack at Pearl Harbor, the citizens on San Piedro Island, like most Americans, are whipped into a frenzy of fear concerning their Japanese American neighbors. The most dramatic manifestation of this fear is the incarceration of Japanese Americans in relocation camps, an action that changed the people on San Piedro long after the war's end.

The novel opens in 1954, about nine years after V-E Day, with accused murderer Kabuo Miyamoto, a Japanese American, on trial for the death of Carl Heine, a local fisherman. It is winter, and snow is falling on the community with an energy fueled by the sea wind. As the courtroom proceedings develop over the course of the novel, it is not only Kabuo who seems to be on trial but the entire community as well. Despite the importance of the deliberations on the accused, the trial becomes a means to review all the tragic misunderstandings and bitterness of San Piedro's ethnic division. The death of Heine and the arrest of Kabuo reopen many festering wounds between the American and Japanese American citizens of the island.

One such wound that has not healed concerns the youthful love affair between Ishmael Chambers (named for the melancholic narrator of Herman Melville's *Moby-Dick*) and Hatsue Miyamoto, the wife of the accused murderer. While covering the trial for his local newspaper, Ishmael, as melancholy as his namesake, is brought back to the memories of his forbidden relationship with Hatsue. Adding to Ishmael's discontent is a wound he incurred during his combat duty in the Pacific against the Japanese. "He had only one arm, the left having been amputated ten inches below the shoulder joint, so that he wore the sleeve of his coat pinned up with the cuff fastened to the elbow."[1] At the trial he confronts his former lover, whom he has never gotten over. The snow, falling in seeming defiance of the human conflicts, pushes Ishmael into bittersweet reminiscences of his youth. "He hoped it would snow recklessly and bring to the island the impossible winter purity, so rare and precious, he remembered fondly from his youth" (8).

At the heart of this story is the treatment of the Japanese American community during the early stages of U.S. involvement in World War II, right after the Japanese surprise attack on Pearl Harbor. Heine's father had previously agreed to sell a portion of his land to the family of the accused murderer. In court during the murder trial, Carl's mother (Etta) explains that

[the deal] included a five-hundred-dollar down payment and an eight-year "lease-to-own" contract. Carl [the father] to collect two hundred and fifty dollars every six months, June 30 and December 31, with six and a half percent interest annually. Papers to be held by Carl, another set by Zenhichi, a third set for any inspector [who] wanted to see them. The Miyamotos—this was back in '34, said Etta—couldn't really own land anyway.

They were from Japan, both of them *born* there, and there was this law on the books prevented them. (121)

Mrs. Heine explains that because the law would only allow Japanese Americans born in the United States who were at least twenty years of age to own property, the land could only revert to the oldest son, Kabuo, after the end of the eight-year lease in 1942. However, according to Etta, the Miyamotos were not able to make the last two of sixteen payments (actually, they were only one payment away from satisfying the loan) because they had been incarcerated in relocation camps; unable to work to make money, they were unable to pay off the loan. The Miyamotos had only been given eight days to take care of their business before being sent to the relocation camp.

When her husband dies in 1944, Mrs. Heine sells the property to another member of the community, Ole Jurgensen, and moves into town, sending the Miyamotos' equity to them in their California relocation camp. Etta also relates that despite her dissent, Carl Jr. and Kabuo had been best friends as boys, but all of that was before the war and before the bitterness of Mrs. Heine's cold-hearted refusal to allow the Miyamotos to possess their land. When Kabuo returns from serving his country in 1945, himself a veteran of the Italian campaign, he asks Etta to return his family's land to them, but she refuses even to discuss the matter.

This disagreement over ownership of that land is what the prosecution theorizes is Kabuo's motive for murdering Carl Jr., especially since Jurgensen eventually agrees to resell the land to Carl right before the murder. The prosecution theorizes that Kabuo murdered Carl out of revenge for taking his family's land again. Carl had beaten Kabuo to the property only by a few hours; Jurgensen had not even had time to take down the For Sale sign. After all, the prosecution asserts, three different fishermen reported seeing Kabuo's boat near Carl's boat on the night of the murder. Kabuo had to have done it. In the end, however, the facts of the matter prove that Carl's death had indeed been an accident—it turns out that on the day of the murder he and Kabuo had agreed to return the property to the Miyamoto family.

Another element in the story concerning the relocation of the Japanese Americans in this community is the separation of Hatsue and Ishmael—the star-crossed lovers. The bitterness of their breakup (initiated by Hatsue's family, who forbade her to continue the relationship) darkens Ishmael's entire life. He can neither forget nor forgive her; his heart has turned cold like the snow. However, because the trial has thrown them back together, he is eventually able to reconcile his bitter experience and his loss. Ironically, it is Ishmael who saves Hatsue's husband from conviction by proving that Carl's death was accidental—the result of his boat being swamped by the wake of a much larger boat. It turns out that Carl's boat had lost electrical power due to a weak battery and that Kabuo had stopped to help him. (This is when the two men agreed to the return of the property.) After Kabuo loaned Carl a spare battery, Carl recklessly attempted to save the old, rusted lantern lashed to his ship's mast, which was about to be destroyed by the wake of an approaching ship. His head was crushed from the fall when the wake hit before he could climb down safely from the mast. Ironically, this act of parsimony on Carl's part, a trait inherited from his mother, dooms him to death. Ishmael reports his evidence to the trial judge, and the case is dismissed.

Because it forces him to exorcise his bitterness over his lost love, Ishmael's saving of Hatsue's husband also ends up saving himself as well. Although he withholds the evidence of Kabuo's innocence for several days while he wrestles with his conscience, he eventually does the right thing. Ishmael's action to save the man who separates him from his true love propels him out of the moral inertia he has maintained since the breakup of his relationship with Hatsue many years earlier.

The accidental death of Carl not only put an innocent man on trial, it also put Ishmael and the entire community on trial for its past transgression. Ironically, Carl's death, as sad as it was for his family, is the catalyst for the reconciliation of past wrongs, an act of atonement for the sins of the community that sent the Japanese Americans to relocation camps. The book ends with Ishmael writing the final report of the story for the newspaper. Although he has not extrinsically gained anything in the novel, Ishmael seems reconciled to his fate, finally devoid of the bitterness that was so prevalent in the beginning:

> Well, thought Ishmael, bending over his typewriter, his fingertips poised just above the keys: the palpitations of Kabuo Miyamoto's heart were unknowable finally. And Hatsue's heart wasn't knowable, either, nor was Carl Heine's. The heart of *any* other, because it had a will, would remain forever mysterious.
>
> Ishmael gave himself to the writing of it, and as he did so he understood this, too: that accident ruled every corner of the universe except the chambers of the human heart. (460)

Although the novel ends like it begins with Ishmael alone, he has at least learned that the human heart is just as capable of doing good as doing evil. In this knowledge he discovers that he has no one to blame, no one to hate, for his losses. Ishmael regains his humanity.

This well-crafted novel illustrates the tragic consequences of the wartime treatment of the Japanese Americans by the U.S. government. The relocation of these citizens not only deprived them of their homes and livelihoods but permanently damaged their lives. This story is just one example of what happened to innocent people during the time when Americans, temporally overcome by fear, acted contrary to the principles of freedom and fairness. But as the novel's title suggests, the power of nature endures in spite of the foibles of flawed humanity. Snows will fall on cedars forever.

Like Greene's *Summer of My German Soldier*, Guterson's evocative novel demonstrates that during World War II the dangers' abounded for individuals no matter where they happened to live.

Note

1. David Guterson, *Snow Falling on Cedars* (New York: Vintage, 1995), 7. All subsequent quotations of this text come from this source.

In *Cedars*, the weathered and weary defense lawyer Nels Gudmundsson (based, it is said, on Guterson's own father, also a defense attorney) argues that Kabuo Miyamoto is simply on trial for being Japanese. "Let fate, coincidence, and accident conspire," Nels tells the jury. "Human beings must act on reason." It feels like one of those scenes where the author, for all intents and purposes, is speaking. Not unlike the righteous words of Atticus Finch, in Harper Lee's *To Kill a Mockingbird*, a novel that Guterson has a famed affection for. Prejudice is irrational, Guterson seems to say; overcome it with reason.

All well and good, but as thinkers from Rousseau on down have noted, reason and rationality have their downfalls. If this is Guterson indulging his desire to preach, so be it, because throughout Cedars he exhibits exemplary evenhandedness with his characters, aware that the passions of hate—and love—will inevitably be unreasonable. Guterson nearly makes the anti-Japanese sentiment of at least some of Cedars' characters understandable. Not rational, of course, certainly not fair: Kabuo, after all, fought for the Allies and (ironically) is haunted by the Germans he killed at war. This while he's disliked by locals with distinctly Germanic names.

"Harmony, like a following breeze at sea, is the exception," an epigraph to *Cedars* reads. Guterson limned this conflict deftly—not only between cultures but also the more universal struggle between passion and rationality.

(...)

So, what are the strengths of *East of the Mountains*? There are several. Most unlikely, perhaps, is that baby-boomer Guterson, with just two novels, has captured something vital and precious—and certainly original—about the World War II experience. The battlefield passages, like the internment scenes in *Cedars*, crackle with relevance and drama.

(...)

The more fascinating aspect of *East of the Mountains* is the seeming dance of acknowledgment and rejection Guterson is performing with the Hemingway of *A Farewell to Arms*—a novel of love and war that also concludes with a birth, although both Frederic's beloved Catherine and the newborn die. Much has been written about Hemingway's archetypical lovers. Leslie Fiedler famously commented that Catherine's death implies Frederic's (and Hemingway's) submerged fear, even loathing, of women, that they can attain nobility only in death, lest they become mother or nag.

This view has been challenged, but in Ben's pained longing for his dead wife, Guterson gives us lovers who are less star-crossed yet just as profound and powerful. "Even after fifty years ... [Ben] celebrated what he'd been granted.... When they'd argued or carried some silent grievance or were divided temporarily by ill-chosen words—still Ben clung to her."

Their love made the long journey. Hence the sad, simple beauty of Rachel's long-standing wish: that upon their death, they would be buried under red and white rosebushes, which she hopes will eventually mingle into a single pink rosebush. "There was no guarantee of pink, they decided. ... They would have their ashes interred side by side, leaving the rest to fate." And Ben admits, in the end, that this perhaps baseless hope may be what steers him away from suicide, so that he can live to speak the novel's final, Odyssean words: "I'm home."

Grace under pressure

At one point Ben is described as an "old man fallen from grace." As depicted by Guterson, however, Ben actually exhibits much of Hemingway's famed "grace under pressure," but it is a pressure of the domestic and mundane, as well as of war and the wilds.

Of course there are stumbles, petty and profound. But I would say the ultimate strength of the two novels is the depth and decency Guterson grants his characters. Writers such as Tom Wolfe and, more recently, Kurt Anderson, of *Turn of the*

Century fame, are lauded for capturing our moment, right down to the way we talk.

If "we" were all urban power brokers in publishing or finance, these accolades might be correct. But Guterson's characters come closer to a universal we—meaning they could be northwesterners in the 1990s or '50s, or Nova Scotians in 1720. As powerful a role as specific historical events play, they seem secondary to the people who struggle with them. A poignant passage from *Cedars* describes Hatsue as "in the stream of history…. She must travel in it easily or her own heart would devour her and she would not endure the war unwounded, as she still hoped to do." This is Guterson at his best, capturing whatever wars we all must confront—fully aware of adversity and its consequences, striving nonetheless.

(...)

JAY CARR ON THE CINEMATIC ADAPTATION

Somber, velvety, haunting, "Snow Falling on Cedars" is a film with the same gravitational pull as the compelling novel on which it's based. A series of interlocking mysteries, it begins in fog, with the death of a fisherman in the Pacific Northwest in 1950. It ends with the clearing away of actual and metaphysical fog and the unlocking of a single chamber in a single human heart. In between, it transports us to a magical world arising from novelist David Guterson's longtime residence on Bainbridge Island in Puget Sound. The fictionalized island and its environs, where life gets pretty primal among the fishing and berry-picking locals, is a character, too, in a film populated by figures who all leave an imprint.

In short, "Snow Falling on Cedars" is the kind of richly layered film that Hollywood seldom attempts, much less brings off. But it's more than brought off here in grand, solid style and beautifully crafted detail by director Scott Hicks. In his first project since "Shine," perhaps Hicks's most remarkable achievement is his ability to make us feel the things haunting the island and its Anglo and Japanese-American populations. The man put on trial for the fisherman's murder is an angry Japanese-American war veteran whose return to town scratches at the consciences of locals who stood by and in some cases even profited when Japanese-Americans were rounded up and removed to internment camps during World War II.

There are several kinds of guilt under the microscope here, including the feelings arising from a forbidden love between the son of the island's idealistic newspaper editor and the Japanese girl he loved and lost to the man who now is on trial. Will Ishmael, Ethan Hawke's young reporter, follow up leads with full diligence? The idealism of his late father, inscribed warmly, trenchantly, and with impressive economy by Sam Shepard, is at war with his unwillingness to let go of his memories of the only woman he loved (Youki Kudoh as Hatsue)—and could not love fully because of the racism that was bigger than both of them. The courtroom issues, personal issues, and larger social issues swirl transfixingly across the screen, emerging from internal and external sources, flitting through several time periods.

This resonant film, with its Stygian blackness and grave clarity, is also reflective and will cause audiences to reflect as well on their country's wartime racism.

(...)

Works by David Guterson

The Country Ahead of Us, The Country Behind, 1989.

"When Schools Fail Children: An English Teacher Educates His Kids at Home." *Harper's,* November 1990: 58–64.

Family Matters: Why Home Schooling Makes Sense, 1992.

"Blood Brothers." *Los Angeles Times,* 1 May 1994: 26+.

Snow Falling on Cedars, 1994.

"Surrounded by Water." *The Earth at Our Doorstep.* Ed. Annie Stine. San Francisco: Sierra Club Books, 1996. 54–61.

East of the Mountains, 1999.

Our Lady of the Forest, 2003.

Annotated Bibliography

Alexander, Joseph H. *Utmost Savagery: The 3 Days of Tarawa.* Naval Institute Press, 1995.

A detailed historical and military account of the three-day battle of Tarawa atoll, including brief personal histories of key military personnel, eyewitness accounts, and battlefield maps.

Armor, John and Peter Wright. *Manzanar.* Photographs by Ansel Adams. New York: Times Books, 1988.

Examines, through photography, life in Manzanar, a Japanese/Japanese American internment camp. Interspersed among the 100 photographs in this collection are interviews with individuals who served time at Manzanar and a brief historical overview of the internment.

Chan, Sucheng. "Changing Fortunes, 1941 to 1965" in *Asian Americans: An Interpretative History.* New York: Simon & Schuster Macmillian, 1991: 121–144.

Provides an in-depth chronology and history of events and policies that have shaped Asian/Asian American experiences in the United States. From immigration to citizenship, Chan's text examines the impact of law, prejudice, and social movements on Asian American populations. This particular chapter deals specifically with the Japanese/Japanese American internment and its aftermath.

Chang, Thelma. *"I Can Never Forget": Men of the 100th/442nd.* Tucson: University of Arizona Press, 1996.

Examines the experiences of the Japanese American (Nisei) soldiers in World War II using photographs and interviews from those who served. Though focused primarily on the narratives of Japanese American soldiers from Hawaii, the text does provide an insider's perspective of life on the battlefield.

Daniels, Roger. *Prisoners Without Trial: Japanese Americans in World War II*. Hill & Wang Pub, 1993.

A concise account that explores the history of discrimination and racial tensions that led to the Japanese/Japanese American internment during World War II. This is one of several books Daniels has written about the internment.

Duus, Peter. *Unlikely Liberators: The Men of the 100th and 442nd*. Masayo Umezawa Duus (translator). University of Hawaii Press, 1989.

A thorough and well-researched book centered on the experiences of second generation Japanese American (Nisei) soldiers in World War II. Included in this text are side stories, personal accounts, and historical overviews.

Gesenway, Deborah and Mindy Roseman. *Beyond Words: Images from America's Concentration Camps*. Ithaca: Cornell University Press, 1987.

Includes reproductions of artwork found in several Japanese/Japanese American internment camps. Gesenway and Roseman supplement the 75 artworks reprinted in *Beyond Words* with excerpted and full interviews with surviving artists who were interned in the camps.

Haystock, Kathy. *David Guterson's Snow Falling on Cedars: A Reader's Guide*. New York: Continuum International Publishing Group Inc., 2002.

A comprehensive guide that includes information about the author, the reception of the novel at the time of publication and its contemporary cultural position, a literary analysis of the novel, and an extended bibliography that includes newspaper articles and interviews about the author.

Hogan, Kathy. *Cohassett Beach Chronicles: World War II in the Pacific Northwest*. Corvallis, Oregon: Oregon State University Press, 1995.

An autobiographical account of life in the Pacific Northwest during World War II, this work considers the role the war played in the lives of those living in Oregon. Focused primarily on the experiences of non-Japanese/Japanese American individuals living in the Pacific Northwest, this text includes newspaper editorials written during World War II.

Houston, Jeanne Wakatsuki and James D. Houston. *Farewell to Manzanar*. Boston: Houghton Mifflin, 1973.

An autobiographical childhood account of life in the Manzanar internment camp.

Inada, Lawson Fusao ed. *Only What We Could Carry: The Japanese American Internment Experience*. Heyday Books, 2000.

A recent collection of Japanese/Japanese American internment experiences. Personal documents, art, and propaganda supplement autobiographical excerpts written by internees.

Irons, Peter. *Justice At War: The Story of the Japanese American Internment Cases*. Berkeley, CA: University of California Press, 1983.

A comprehensive historical text that closely examines four Supreme Court cases in which Japanese American citizens attempted to challenge the constitutionality of the internment. Included in this work are legal briefs, courtroom testimonies, and Supreme Court rulings.

Kessler, Lauren. *Stubborn Twig: Three Generations in the Life of a Japanese American Family*. New York: Penguin, 1993.

A detailed social history of a Japanese/Japanese American family in Oregon. Kessler's work spans three generations, from the turn of the 19th century to the Japanese American internment, and includes familial interviews.

Kogawa, Joy. *Obasan*. New York: Anchor Books, 1994.

A fictional account of the internment of Japanese Canadians during World War II.

Lee, Harper. *To Kill a Mockingbird*. Philadelphia: Lippincott, 1960.

A fictional account of life in a segregated Southern town prior to the rise of the Civil Rights Movement, this novel explores the ways in which prejudice and racism function in a particular community. Lee's work structurally and thematically influenced David Guterson's *Snow Falling on Cedars*, and it is, in reviews of *Snow Falling on Cedars* and in interviews with the Guterson, a consistent foundation for comparison and critique.

Mackey, Mike ed. *Remembering Heart Mountain: Essays on Japanese American Internment in Wyoming*. Powell, WY: Western History Publications, 1998.

A collection of nonfiction essays written about the Japanese American internment camp in Wyoming. This collection was written in conjunction with the Heart Mountain symposium held in Powell in 1995, the 50th anniversary of the closing of the camp.

Nakasone, Edwin. *The Nisei Soldier: Historical Essays on World War II*. White Bear Lake, MN: J-Press, 1997.

Drawing upon his own experience as a second generation Japanese American (Nisei) soldier in the United States Army, Nakasone supplements his narrative of World War II with interviews with other Nisei soldiers. Also included in this historical collection of World War II narratives are stories that represent the Japanese perspective on the war.

Okada, John. *No-No Boy*. University of Washington Press, 1980. (Originally published by Charles E. Tuttle, Rutherford, Vermont, and Tokyo, Japan, 1957).

A post-World War II fictional account about the experiences of Japanese and Japanese Americans living in the Pacific Northwest. Ichiro, a Japanese American who was interned, along with his family, during World War II, is the protagonist. The title of the novel comes from the protagonist's refusal to serve in the United States military, and it is this act of resistance, and its consequences, that serves as one of the primary foundations for the novel's plot.

Okihiro, Gary Y. and Joan Myers. *Whispered Silences: Japanese Americans and World War II.* Seattle: University of Washington Press, 1996.

A collaborative photographic essay about the Japanese/Japanese American internment. In 1981, photographer Myers visited the remains of Manzanar, which prompted a more extensive exploration of 9 other internment camps. 65 duotone photographs of landscapes and discarded objects are included in this collection.

Okihiro, a third generation Japanese American (sansei) historian, uses poetry, memories of internees, and his father's experiences during World War II as the textual basis for the essays that accompanies the images.

Okubo, Mine. *Citizen 13660.* reprinted by University of Washington Press, 1983. Originally published by Columbia University Press, 1946.

One of the earliest narratives about the internment, *Citizen 13660* is a first-hand account of life in the Japanese/Japanese American internment camps. Okubo, who was a college student at the time of her family's forced relocation, includes daily accounts of every day life and illustrations.

Snow Falling on Cedars: The Shooting Script. New York: Newmarket Press, 1999.

Includes a full-length film script of *Snow Falling on Cedars*, photographs of the Japanese/Japanese American internment, stills from the film, and commentaries by director Scott Hicks.

Takaki, Ronald. *Strangers from a Different Shore: A History of Asian Americans.* New York: Little, Brown and Company, 1989.

Examines the 150 year history of Asians and Asian Americans in the United States, with a focus on labor, poverty, and prejudice. This broad, multi-ethnic survey includes interviews, historical documents, and photographs. Specific reference to the experiences of Japanese/Japanese Americans during World War II can be found in Chapter 10, pp. 357–405, entitled "The Watershed of World War II: Democracy and Race."

Tateishi, John ed. *And Justice for All: An Oral History of the Japanese American Detention Camps.* University of Washington Press: 1984.

A collection of interviews of Japanese/Japanese American internees.

Yamamoto, Hisaye. *Seventeen Syllables and Other Stories.* New Brunswick, N.J. Rutgers University Press, 1994.

A collection of fictional and memoir accounts of Japanese/Japanese American experience in the United States. Included in this collection are stories about the Japanese/Japanese American internment.

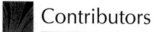 Contributors

HAROLD BLOOM is Sterling Professor of the Humanities at Yale University and Henry W. and Albert A. Berg Professor of English at the New York University Graduate School. He is the author of over 20 books, including *Shelley's Mythmaking* (1959), *The Visionary Company* (1961), *Blake's Apocalypse* (1963), *Yeats* (1970), *A Map of Misreading* (1975), *Kabbalah and Criticism* (1975), *Agon: Toward a Theory of Revisionism* (1982), *The American Religion* (1992), *The Western Canon* (1994), and *Omens of Millennium: The Gnosis of Angels, Dreams, and Resurrection* (1996). *The Anxiety of Influence* (1973) sets forth Professor Bloom's provocative theory of the literary relationships between the great writers and their predecessors. His most recent books include *Shakespeare: The Invention of the Human* (1998), a 1998 National Book Award finalist, *How to Read and Why* (2000), *Genius: A Mosaic of One Hundred Exemplary Creative Minds* (2002), and *Hamlet: Poem Unlimited* (2003). In 1999, Professor Bloom received the prestigious American Academy of Arts and Letters Gold Medal for Criticism, and in 2002 he received the Catalonia International Prize.

CATHY SCHLUND-VIALS is a doctoral student in the American Studies Program in the Department of English at the University of Massachusetts-Amherst. Her fields of research include immigration narratives at the turn of the century and post-1965, Ethnic Studies, and Asian American Studies. She is currently the Program Curator for New WORLD Theater, a multicultural theater company in residence at the University of Massachusetts.

MICHAEL HARRIS is a regular contributor and book reviewer for the *Los Angeles Times*.

PICO IYER is an essayist and author who is a frequent contributor to *Time* magazine and *Travelers' Tales Japan*. He has published several travel narratives, including *Video Night in Kathmandu: And Other Reports from the Not-so-far East* (1988), *The Lady and the Monk: Four Seasons in Kyoto* (1991), *Falling off the Map: Some Lonely Places of the World* (1993), *Tropical Classical: Essays from Several Directions* (1997), and *The Global Soul: Jet Lag, Shopping Malls, and the Search for Home* (2000). He is also the author of *The Recovery of Innocence* (1984), *Cuba and the Night* (1995), and *Abandon A Romance* (2003).

SUSAN KENNEY is the Dana Professor of Creative Writing at Colby College. She received her B.A. from Northwestern University and her M.A. and Ph.D. from Cornell University. She has taught at Colby College since 1968. She has published several books, including *Garden of Malice* (1983), *In Another Country: A Novel* (1984), *Graves in Academe* (1985), *Sailing* (1987), *One Fell Sloop* (1990), and *Murder in the Wind: A Mystery Jigsaw Puzzle* (1993). She is also a frequent contributor to *The New York Times*.

CAROL HERMAN is a writer living in Maryland. She is a frequent reviewer of contemporary fiction for the *Washington Times*.

NANCY PATE is a founding member of the Southern Book Critics' Circle and has received the Robin Mays award given by the Publishers Association of the South. She co-authored *Fiddle Dee Death*, under the nom de plume of Caroline Cousins, along with Meg Herndon and Gail Greer. Pate lives in Orlando, Florida, where she is the book critic for the *Orlando Sentinel*.

LUCY HUGHES-HALLETT is an award-winning journalist and author whose work has appeared in *Vogue*, the *London Evening Standard*, and the *Sunday Times*. She has received the Catherine Pakenham Award for journalism (1980), the Emily Toth Award (1991), and the Fawcett Book Prize (1992). She is the author of *Cleopatra: Histories, Dreams, and Distortions*, an in-depth examination of the Egyptian queen.

JANE MENDELSOHN is the author of *I Was Amelia Earhart* (1996), which spent fourteen weeks on the *New York Times* bestseller list and was published in fifteen languages. Her most recently published novel is *Innocence* (2001). She has contributed book reviews to the *Village Voice* and *Manchester Guardian Weekly*.

SUZANNE MANTELL is a freelance writer based in Los Angeles. Her book reviews and articles have appeared in the *Utne Reader*, *Los Angeles Times*, and *Publishers Weekly*.

JUDITH BROMBERG teaches high school English in Kansas City, Missouri. She is a frequent book reviewer for the *National Catholic Reporter*.

JAMES H. MEREDITH is Associate Professor of English at the United States Air Force Academy.

TOM DEIGNAN teaches English, history, and film at City University of New York. He is also an editor and columnist at The Irish Voice. He is currently at work on a novel called *Staten Islanders*.

JAY CARR has been the film critic of the *Boston Globe* since 1983. He is also the editor of *The A List: The National Film society of Film Critics' 100 Essential Films*, which was published in 2002.

Acknowledgments

I want to first thank Jennifer Ho for pointing me in the direction of this project, and I would like to extend a special thanks to Sue Naab at Chelsea House Publishers for her patience, advice, and guidance. I am grateful to Bridget Marshall for her support and her editing assistance. And, I am indebted to my husband, Christopher Vials, an invaluable colleague and my closest friend.

"Sometimes Even Good People Must Coexist With Evil" by Michael Harris. From *Los Angeles Times*, September 19, 1994, p. E4. © 1994 by The Times Mirror Company. Reprinted by permission.

"Snowbound: On a Remote Island, a Vivid Tale of Clashing Cultures" by Pico Iyer. From *Time* 144, No. 13 (26 September 1994), 79. © 1994 by *Time*. Reprinted by permission.

"Their Fellow Americans" by Susan Kenney. From *The New York Times Book Review*, October 16, 1994, pp. 12–13. © 1994 by *The New York Times Book Review*. Reprinted by permission.

"*Snow Falling* Does Justice to Trial Fiction" by Carol Herman. From *The Washington Times*, October 23, 1994, p. B7. © 1994 by *The Washington Times*. Reprinted by permission.

"Murder Unveils an Island's Secrets" by Nancy Pate. From *Chicago Tribune*, January 12, 1995,: p. 4. Originally published in the *Orlando Sentinel*, December 25, 1994. ©1994 by the *Orlando Sentinel*. Reprinted by permission.

"Looking Like the Enemy" by Lucy Hughes–Hallett. From *Sunday Times*, May 28, 1995, Features section. © 1995 by *Sunday Times*. Reprinted by permission.

Index

summary and analysis, 20–62
and *To Kill a Mockingbird*, 7
treatment of the Japanese
   American community, 81–82
trials impact on those in the
   courtroom, 50–51
and use of memory, 78–80

T
To Kill a Mockingbird (Lee),
   and *Snow Falling on Cedars*, 7

W
Whaley, Horace, in *Snow Falling
   on Cedars*
   character summary, 16
   testimony of, 24–25